# Thomas Hardy

# Thomas Hardy

Tim Dolin

HAUS PUBLISHING · LONDON

First published in Great Britain in 2008 by
Haus Publishing Limited
26 Cadogan Court
Draycott Avenue
London SW3 3BX

**www.hauspublishing.co.uk**

Copyright © Tim Dolin, 2008

The moral rights of the author have been asserted

A CIP catalogue record for this book is available from the British Library

ISBN 978-1-904950-77-6

Typeset in Garamond 3 by MacGuru Ltd
*info@macguru.org.uk*

Printed in India by International Print-O-Pac Limited
Front Cover: portrait – Topham Picturepoint; background – Getty Images

# Contents

The statue of Thomas Hardy in Dorchester.

# Introduction: The Stir of the Present

Turn off the A35 early in the morning and make your way into Dorchester. Park near the coach bays in the pay-and-display at the Top o' Town and cross the roundabout where High West Street begins its long, steep, straight descent past St Peter's, the Corn Exchange, and down towards Grey's Bridge and the water-meadows of the Frome at the bottom. If you arrive early enough the street is empty, and still in shadow from the well-preserved Georgian and Victorian stone buildings along each side. It's not hard to imagine yourself remote, as Virginia Woolf once said of Thomas Hardy, from 'the stir of the present and its littleness'.[1] This, you feel certain, is the heart of Wessex, the still centre of Hardy's *partly real, partly dream-country*[2] which stretches out from the county town into the pastures, chalk downs and heathland surrounding it: a *province bounded on the north by the Thames, on the south by the English Channel, on the east by a line running from Hayling Island to Windsor Forest, and on the west by the Cornish coast.*[3]

Just as you are about to make your way down the hill, you notice out of the corner of your eye a statue in the leafy shade to the left of the roundabout. Incongruously, it faces the other way, towards the car-park. Unusually, too, for a piece of memorial sculpture, it is exactly life-sized, and seems as a result much too small. It depicts a kindly old man dressed for the outdoors in breeches, holding a hat, sitting passively with legs crossed and eyes lowered, lost in thought among the heathland plants sculpted around his boots. As if to answer your question, the plaque near Eric Kennington's statue of Hardy explains that this unpropitious 'site would have appealed to [its subject] because it stands upon old Roman walls and is close to the very centre of the Dorchester he knew, loved, and immortalized in his novel *The Mayor of Casterbridge* (1886)'. Certainly the odd placement of the statue, close to the centre but somehow out of its orbit, emulates Hardy's own reticence and modesty – as it does the ambivalence many local people felt (and still feel) towards their town's most famous upstart.[4] But it is also somehow an aptly, profoundly *Hardyan* memorial. It is not only that Kennington's sympathetic likeness recalls Somerset Maugham's description of Hardy as 'a little man with an earthy face [and] a strange look of the soil'.[5] Here, too, is someone who seems not altogether at home on his plinth: whose reserve made him feel self-conscious and uncertain of his place of honour, and whose class sensitivity made him acutely uneasy about his right to such a display.

Think of Hardy and you think of the past: the world before motor cars, aeroplanes, TVs, mobile phones or email. Looking down the empty High Street, you are reassured that here life was once slower, more grounded, more connected. You read *Jude the Obscure*, as Sven Birkerts did in his bestselling complaint on the decline of reading, *The Gutenberg Elegies* (1994), because it is a 'window opening upon *how it was*'. You want to know, like Birkerts, how 'Jude's world is different from ours'. As you read the novel, your 'sense of silence deepens. No background hum, no ambient noise. When people communicate, it is face to face. Or else by letter. There are no telephones or cars to hurriedly bridge the spatial gaps. We hear voices and we hear footsteps die away in the distance. Days pass at a pace we can hardly imagine. A letter arrives and it is an event. The sound of paper unfolding, of wind in the trees outside the door. And then the things, their *thingness*'.[6] Reading Hardy lets Birkerts retrieve a past world, and experience something retrievable now *only* through reading: an experience of time – he calls it 'duration' – and real contact with material life. In electronic postmodernity we may be able to communicate faster, but we have paid the price, in 'a reduced attention span and a general impatience with sustained inquiry; … a shattered faith in institutions and in the explanatory narratives that formerly gave shape to subjective experience; … a divorce from the past, from a vital sense of history as a cumulative or organic process; … an estrangement from geographic place and community; and … an absence of any strong vision of a personal or collective future'.[7]

But has Birkerts really made contact with Hardy in his deep, quiet place? For the world of electronic postmodernity he describes is also unintentionally a description of the world of *Jude the Obscure*, the story of a man and a woman who, like so many of Hardy's heroes and heroines, are born outside their time. Jude Fawley and Sue Bridehead are the survivors of old social formations left almost extinct by modernity, and they are *deracinés* moderns. They are excluded by class prejudice from education and social success, outlawed by outmoded conventions of marriage, and driven almost to madness by the cultural and symbolic force of a Christianity no longer capable of commanding spiritual authority. This, too, is Hardy's Wessex.

How is it, then, that we can be so comforted by Hardy's writing – so nostalgic for its lost world, so much in need of its rustic sim-plicity – when it quite clearly confronts us, without sentimentality and *without a mincing of words*, with the present: our own present as well as Hardy's *modern Wessex of railways, the penny post, mowing and reaping machines, union workhouses, lucifer matches, labourers who could read and write, and National school children*?[8] Hardy rightly belongs, we like to think, in an ancient landscape shaped by the remains of Bronze Age burial-mounds built on the high hilltops so that the dead could watch over the living in the valleys below;[9] a changeless landscape where the old life-ways *will go onward the same / Though*

*Dynasties pass.*[10] More than 30 years ago the critic and novelist Raymond Williams challenged this conventional view of Hardy. Williams recognized in Wessex a place that was still intimately and painfully familiar to him in the middle of the 20th century: 'that border country so many of us have been living in', he called it, between customary and educated life.[11] Williams's influence on subsequent understandings of Hardy has been enormous, and over recent decades the myth of the grand old man of Wessex has been slowly dismantled. Hardy is no longer a tragic humanist 'opposing the "old wisdom" of the rural world to the "desolating influences" of "modern civilization"'.[12] He is now viewed as essentially an experimental social novelist. He is no realistic chronicler of social life (although his aim, he said, was to *preserve ... a fairly true record of a vanishing life*[13]). Rather, he is a writer whose particular genius was a product of the complex and contradictory social trajectory of a 'returned native': an eldest son educated out of the modest capital sum his self-employed rural artisan family invested in the rise of the family name, who never quite belonged in metropolitan literary society nor ever felt quite at home again in the villages of his upbringing. Read aright, Hardy is no rural realist, but an alienated proto-modernist, self-consciously aware of the fictiveness of all fiction, who writes about 'a contingent, "senseless" universe in which individuals are out of control of the social forces which exploit and victimize them' and 'characters who are not unified human subjects, but ... inconsistent clusters of "images" of the social and psychological "circumstances" which construct them'.[14]

But the fact remains that Hardy was drawn back irresistibly to the physical and human landscapes of his birthplace. He chose to make them his home and the basis of his art in the full knowledge that his education and social mobility prohibited him from inhabiting them in the unselfconscious way of his family and forebears or his own early childhood days. He no longer quite fitted in, but he knew the place intimately and remembered it intimately, as it was and no longer was. He noticed everything about it, in every season, weather, light; and he read and listened closely to all the stories of its past, intent on committing to paper what had once been committed to local memory. Influenced by the Romantic poets, he showed how the force of imagination can compensate for the losses of modernity. His great achievement was to unite the dream country and the real country. The physical Wessex is a cleared aesthetic space, abstracted from social actuality by the very inalterability of its features, shaped by the land-use and habitation patterns of thousands of years. It is, as Hardy wrote in *The Woodlanders* (1887), *one of those sequestered spots outside the gates of the world where ... from time to time, ... dramas of a grandeur and unity truly Sophoclean are enacted in the real, by virtue of the concentrated passions and closely-knit interdependence of the lives therein.*[15] The landscape takes up the burden of the 'universal', leaving Hardy free to explore that same place in the real – as a largely traumatized social world. By *closely-knit interdependence* he means the social and economic interdependence of rural and urban lives in industrial capitalism, but also the interdependence of those social and economic facts and the concentrated passions of individuals, and their emotions, intellects and wills.

Despite the appearance of Eric Kennington's statue at the Top o'Town, therefore, Hardy was no rustic. He lived, in all, about one-third of his life in London. He first visited the city with his mother as a child, lived there for most of the 1860s and 1870s, and spent several months in residence each year for the next four decades. But his repeated claim that he was virtually a *born Londoner* has been mostly downplayed as a provincial petty-bourgeois man's desire to pass himself off as a sophisticated metropolitan. It is true that he could never forgive the reviewers who, *if he only touched on London in his pages, promptly reminded him not to write of a place he was unacquainted with, but to get back to his sheepfolds.*[16] It is also true that he rarely wrote convincingly about London (in fiction, at least). But Hardy's originality lies in those London years. His mind was shaped by the astonishing new ideas that were throwing intellectual and political life into turmoil there in the 1850s and 1860s – the science of Darwin and the liberalism of Mill. His metropolitan intellect, alive to contemporary debates, complemented the intensely visual imagination that rural life had bred in him. When he finally settled back in Dorchester as a middle-aged man, he described it as his *country-quarters* rather than his home, and foresaw that the town was as convenient as *a London suburb, owing to quick locomotion*.[17] He knew both worlds intimately, and, if he didn't comfortably belong in either, his habit of shuttling between his place of work and leisure became essential to the art he made.

Hardy's physical appearance, which reflected his abstemious lifestyle and appetite for hard work at his desk, was much more that of a professional London man than a countryman, and it took his readers aback. When the younger novelist George Gissing met him at home in 1895 he wrote to a friend: 'I admire Hardy's best work very highly, but in the man himself I feel disappointed.'[18] Short and slim, he was neatly-dressed and upright, with white, soft, squared-off fingers: a man curiously out of place in the open air (he didn't even know the names of the wildflowers in his own fields, Gissing announced incredulously), whose appearance and manner constantly surprised people who saw or met him. In middle age he wore a beard closely trimmed and coming to a point 'after the Elizabethan manner',[19] which gave him the unexpected appearance of the city or town man – a banker, perhaps, or a doctor or lawyer. Ford Madox Ford described it as an 'elder-statesman's beard'. When Hardy shaved it off a few years later in favour of a waxed moustache, it 'stuck out', Ford put it mischievously, 'like that of the sergeant-major of a bantam regiment'.[20] With the exception of his eyes – 'keen, limpid, liquid, poet-peasant's eyes',[21] vulnerable and melancholy: eyes everyone noticed – he 'did not present the idea of a typical literary man'.[22] The cartoonist Leslie Ward ('Spy') recalled his surprise that Hardy's clothes should have 'had a sporting touch about them', and his subsequent cartoon in *Vanity Fair* endows Hardy with an incongruous jauntiness.[23] So too, Edmund Gosse found him as a very old man 'full of spirit and gaiety not quite consistent in the most pessimistic of poets'.[24]

Gosse had known Hardy very well for many years; others who knew him less well found him stiffly formal in conversation, and often distant or ill at ease. He was so painfully shy and self-effacing, 'so needing appreciation',[25] that he constantly took refuge behind the mask of the poet-peasant, hiding his extreme reserve beneath the dreamy detachment of someone 'little interested in his surroundings'[26] and almost incapable of appreciating his own art: the 'village atheist' of G K Chesterton's hurtful jibe. In 1895 Gissing came away with the unaccountable impression that Hardy 'evidently [did] not read very much' and 'sadly need[ed] a larger outlook upon life – a wider culture'.[27] Edith Wharton remembered too that he 'seemed to take little interest in the literary movements of the day, or in fact in any critical discussion of his craft, and I felt he was completely enclosed in his own creative dream, through which I imagine few voices or influences ever reached him'.[28] And when Rupert Brooke met him in 1910, he talked not about his own work but about 'the best manure for turnips'.[29]

For all the facts we have since collected about him, Hardy remains the enigma he was to many of his contemporaries, a man whose visible personality often seemed strangely disconnected from – even alien to – his own writing. Yet how well he understood the mysteriousness of identity. He did not think of himself (or anyone else) as a single individual who could be known conclusively, but as 'various persons'. In a notebook entry from late 1890 he declared: *I am more than ever convinced that persons are successively various persons, according as each special strand in their characters is brought uppermost by circumstances.*[30] And one of his last (and lesser) poems, 'So Various', published posthumously in March 1928, makes a frank public inventory of all the contradictions and inconsistencies in his character: the ardent young idealist, a puppet of his passions, is also the cold fish; the faithful lover is also fickle; the seeming dunce a learned seer; the *man of sadness* is *Indubitably / good company*; the *unadventurous slow man* the *man of enterprise, shrewd and swift* who *might climb* ambitiously to the top. *All these specimens of man*, the poem concludes, *Were* one *man. Yea,/I was all they.*[31]

In 1885 Hardy copied into his notebook a passage from a magazine essay by the novelist Vernon Lee which supported this idea. By 'the fatality of heredity', Lee argued, 'a human being contains within himself a number of different tendencies, all moulded, it is true, into one character, but existing none the less each in its special nature'. But there was more to it than that, Lee suggested, for 'by the fatality of environment every human being is modified in many different ways ... rammed into place until he fits it, & absorbs fragments of all the other personalities with whom he is crushed together'.[32] What follows are some of the various persons Hardy was and became by the fatality of heredity and the fatality of the various environments in which he was born and lived: provincial, professional, novelist, poet, and, ultimately, a cultural institution which was also a holiday destination – the 'Hardy Country'.

Out of these contradictory selves come the variousness and unevenness of Hardy's vast creative output, the 'oddity and idiosyncrasy' of his language, and the greatness of his art.[33] The self-educated son of isolated rural smallholders who conquered London as the greatest writer of his generation, his fundamental social dislocation produced an art at once profoundly insightful about modern social life and lovingly attentive to a richly detailed and dying local culture. He is unique among modern writers in exploring the deracinating experience of modern global capitalism in stories and images of farm, village and town life. He was passionately opposed to the destruction of local cultures and social well-being by massive economic forces, but his life and work show us how, through the power of the imagination, we can connect meaningfully and without nostalgia with *where we are* – with real and virtual landscapes, and local, national and global histories and memories. Few writers of his stature struck such a chord with their contemporaries, and continue to speak to new generations of readers. Hardy wrote about social suffering, sexual freedom, exploitation, unbelief, and the courage and honesty to face the worst; and yet did so in a way that draws us back to a world at once reassuring and disturbing, remote from the stir of the present and yet a characteristic product of it.

# Provincial 1840–62

On 2 June 1840, when Queen Victoria was 21 years old and in the first months of her marriage to Prince Albert, and Lord Melbourne, onetime friend of Shelley and Byron, was in the final months of his last term as prime minister, a premature baby boy was stillborn in the bedroom of an isolated cottage *in a lonely and silent spot between woodland and heathland* near Dorchester, 115 miles south-west of London.[34] Concerned for the survival of the baby's mother – it had been a difficult and dangerous labour – the surgeon hurriedly thrust the corpse out of the way. Only the local midwife, Lizzy Downton, noticed something, and exclaimed: *'Dead! Stop a minute: he's alive enough, sure!'* [35] So it was that Thomas Hardy was born – or, rather, survived his birth. In old age he left a record of the eventful day, burying it, characteristically enough, in the middle of the biography he ended up writing (most of) himself (the *Life*). It is a matter-of-fact description of the workings of fortune: *At his birth he was thrown aside as dead till rescued by* an *estimable woman's commonsense.*[36]

Hardy's view of the world was profoundly shaped by these unpropitious beginnings in it. The frail infant grew only slowly: *he was a child till he was sixteen*, he later explained, *a youth till he was five-and-twenty, and a young man till he was nearly fifty* (this, he believed, was the clue to *much of his character and action throughout his life*).[37] Yet he lived into his 88th year, and entertained Queen Victoria's grandson – then the king-in-waiting – in the garden of

Thomas Hardy as an infant, with his mother Jemima.

his Dorchester home. But he always felt the tenuousness of the human hold upon life, and the determining force of chance, and the lowliness and obscurity of his own birth.

Hardy liked to imagine a romantic history for his lowborn family: a tale of genealogical corruption and decline over the centuries from an illustrious county family to a dynasty of independent artisans – master-masons for four generations, he claimed.[38] He *often thought* that *he would like to restore the 'le' to his name* – a handwritten 'Hardy Pedigree' which he drew up in 1917 makes tenuous links back to some Jersey 'le Hardys' – and he was an avid reader of Hutchins's *History and Antiquities of Dorset* (1774).[39] But Dorset is so full of Hardys that it is impossible to trace the family back with any certainty. Some biographers have claimed that he was a social-climber ashamed of his humble family background.[40] In truth, although his mother, Jemima, was indeed a maid-servant before her marriage (a fact he omitted from the *Life*), her forebears had once been smallholders and professional people in north-west Dorset who had married badly and come down in the world. Jemima Hardy was unquestionably the most significant figure in her son's life. She was, he often said, a woman *of unusual ability and judgment, and an energy that might have carried her to incalculable issues*.[41] Ambitious for her sickly baby boy, she was the model for his own later self-image as a writer, and passed on to him what she had inherited from her own ancestors: their professionalism.

On his father's side, Hardy's great-grandfather, John Hardy of Puddletown, had been a mason who became prosperous enough in 1800 to build a cottage for his son Thomas – the first of three generations of Thomases, confusingly – on two acres of land at Higher Bockhampton (as it became) on the heathland fringes of the Kingston Maurward estate, about three miles from Dorchester. He was granted a lifehold tenancy by the estate (a renewable lease that can be passed down but not disposed of). In 1835 the lifehold was duly extended to Hardy's grandfather Thomas and the two sons of his who had gone into the family business, doing general building work on the estate, including the big house. When Jemima married Thomas Hardy II late in 1839 – she was already pregnant with our Thomas – they both moved in to the cottage with his widowed mother, Mary Hardy. There a sister, also Mary, was born in 1841 (she remained Hardy's closest sibling);

The cottage at Higher Bockhampton where Hardy was born.

and after a space of ten years, a brother, Henry, in 1851, and a baby sister, Kate, in 1856.

The cottage still feels secluded today. Facing west at the end of a lane and surrounded by dense woods, it backs on to what remains of the heath. Hardy's earliest poem, 'Domicilium', records a wild and ancient heathland landscape:

> *Heath and furze*
> *Are everything that seems to grow and thrive*
> *Upon the uneven ground. A stunted thorn*
> *Stands here and there, indeed; and from a pit*
> *An oak uprises, springing from a seed*
> *Dropped by some bird a hundred years ago.*

But as in so much of Hardy's writing, the speaker observes a many-layered scene, dwelt in, worked over and tramped across by generations of local people: a landscape where *change has marked / The face of many things*. 'Domicilium' is a homage to his grandmother

Mary and the *days bygone*. In a much later poem, 'One We Knew', she is remembered as a mesmerizing storyteller holding captive the children who gathered *around her knees* in the cottage to hear tales of old country dances, the maypole, the gibbet, and most of all the French Revolution and the rise of Bonaparte's *unbounded / Ambition and arrogance*:

> *Of how his threats woke warlike preparations*
> > *Along the southern strand,*
> *And how each night brought tremors and trepidations*
> > *Lest morning should see him land.*[42]

History for Hardy had a local geography. Places intimately known were alive with the past. Those who dwelled there had *an almost exhaustive biographical or historical acquaintance with every object, animate and inanimate, within {their} horizon.*[43] The Napoleonic past seemed very near indeed: less than half a mile from the cottage, the burial mound of Rainbarrow at the top of Duddle Heath had served as a signal beacon during those warlike preparations. The excitement and danger of the crisis, so vividly recounted by his grandmother, remained with Hardy for the rest of his life. He was fascinated by the Napoleonic period, and by the idea it evoked of a shattering collision between ordinary men and women living in old settlements deep in the remote countryside and the great historical forces that would suddenly thrust them to the centre of the world's affairs. So profound was this fascination that T E Lawrence, a neighbour and friend, observed how in very old age Napoleon had become 'a real man to [Hardy], and the country of Dorsetshire echoes that name everywhere in [his] ears. He lives in his period, and thinks of it as the great war'.[44] He had begun to dwell, as his grandmother did, on *dead themes, not as one who remembers,/ But rather as one who sees.*[45]

Old Mary Hardy was a vital link back to the oral traditions

and cultural memory of the family and local community; Jemima was the dominant personality and driving force in the family, as well as a fund of stories and folk wisdom herself. But Hardy's father was also, in his own way, an important influence. He was a vigorous handsome man with *a quick step and a habit of bearing his head a little to one side as he walked. He carried no stick or umbrella till past middle-life, and was altogether an open-air liver, and a great walker always.*[46] Where Jemima was a person of great intensity – dynamic, formidable, fatalistic, strong-willed, fiercely outspoken – her husband was (or was characterized by his family to be) her very opposite: an easygoing and charming man without much ambition or force of personality. He was a musician who played violin with the small band of musicians that made up the 'choir' in the gallery of the local parish church at Stinsford, including his father and uncle. The Hardys were the leading figures until the new vicar, Arthur Shirley, replaced them with a barrel organ under acrimonious circumstances in the early 1840s. Like the Mellstock choir in *Under the Greenwood Tree* – based closely on the Stinsford players and their demise – they remained in demand to play at local dances, wedding feasts and other celebrations, as well as the local rounds of Christmas carolling. Hardy was a delicate child *of ecstatic temperament* who remained *extraordinarily sensitive to music* all his life.[47] In the evenings, the cottage was filled with his father's playing, and the little boy danced alone *in the middle of the room*, enraptured, to the *jigs, hornpipes, reels, waltzes, and country-dances.*[48] Soon afterwards he learned the violin himself, and played along at many of the local parties.

Hardy's father was a reserved and receptive man who tended to stay in the background, looking on and leaving Jemima to be the voice of the family. His son inherited something of that quiet, curious observer's eye. Hardy recalled how his father *liked going alone into the woods or on the heath, where, with a telescope ... he would stay peering into the distance by the half-hour; or, in the hot weather, lying on a bank of thyme or camomile with the grasshoppers leaping over him.*[49] Significantly, two of the clearest memories Hardy had of his own childhood and youth were closely related to these leisurely recreations of his father's. In the first, the young boy *was lying on his back in the sun, thinking how useless he was, and covered his face with his straw hat. The sun's rays streamed through the interstices of the straw,* causing him to reflect how *he did not want to be a man, or to possess things, but to remain as he was, in the same spot.* Naturally, this *early evidence of a lack of social ambition which followed him through life* was deeply hurtful to his mother, who *never forgot what he had said.*[50] Nor did Hardy forget. When as an old man he looked back on the critical junctures in his life, he invariably saw them as the outcome of an internalized war of temperaments. One was forward looking, open to change, shrewd, alert to opportunities for social advancement: the *man of enterprise* of 'So Various'. The other was backward looking, indecisive and reluctant to act, resistant to innovation, regretful of lost habits and customs: the *unadventurous slow man.*[51]

Another vivid memory is of a morning a few years later when Hardy took his father's telescope up onto the heath, focusing it on Dorchester, three miles away, where a man was to be hanged. *At the moment of his placing the glass to his eye the white figure dropped downwards, and the faint note of the town clock struck eight.* Shocked, *the glass nearly fell from Hardy's hands. He seemed alone on the heath with the hanged man, and crept homeward wishing he had not been so curious.*[52] Here, compressed into one of Hardy's distinctive and striking visual tableaux, is a drama present in so much of his writing: the shameful secretiveness of the onlooker 'beset' by what he sees, finding himself no longer uninvolved even from his safe distance.[53] But this was only *the second ... execution he witnessed, the first having been that of a woman two or three years earlier, when he stood close to the gallows*: Martha Brown. The eager 16-year-old Hardy must have arrived very early to secure a place near the front of a crowd of 3–4,000 people, and he was, as he later disarmed his listeners by implying, guiltily aroused by the swinging body, tight in its rain-soaked *black silk gown*.[54]

He may not have been an ambitious man, but Thomas Hardy senior was moderately successful in maintaining and expanding the family business. He was fortunate in inheriting it at the beginning of a period of enormous social upheaval and, ultimately, emerging prosperity in England. During the hungry 1840s there were times when the Hardys lived from hand to mouth. But as the decade progressed, the effects of fundamental nationwide economic reforms began to be felt. The most significant of these was the phased repeal of the Corn Laws beginning in 1846, which stripped away the trade protection from which the agricultural sector and the landed classes had benefited since the Napoleonic period, and transformed British agriculture into a free-trading economy. The Hardys, running a small family business founded on their artisan skills, were staunch free-traders who welcomed the repeals of the Corn Laws, and they were among those who reaped the rewards. From being effectively a self-employed bricklayer in the 1840s, Thomas Hardy senior employed six men in the more vigorous economic conditions in 1861, and eight men and a boy in 1871: this despite his son's observation that he *did not possess the art of enriching himself by business*.[55]

The success of the family concern, and the revolution in rural daily life that was beginning to take place everywhere around Dorchester, were decisive factors in shaping Hardy. He has rightly been called the great 'transitional' British writer – a Victorian modern – but he is, more profoundly, the child of a late phase of that long, traumatic period of social transition in the English countryside that began with industrialization in the 18th century. Hardy's experience was unique among English novelists in that he grew up in a county where modernization occurred relatively late – compared with the Midlands counties, for instance – and within what remained largely an agricultural economy. As a result, enormous social changes were compressed into the experience of a single generation of people whose lives seemed outwardly little different. The railway came to Dorchester in 1847, standardizing time and slaying *the orally transmitted ditties of centuries* with *London comic songs*.[56] One of its functions, as Tess Durbeyfield knew, was to deliver food from agricultural regions to the cities. In the 1840s the rate of enclosure and the mechanization of agricultural work accelerated to meet the needs of rapidly increasing urban populations, and these changes forced out many of the labouring families who had depended on a small plot of land to raise chickens and vegetables to supplement their meagre wages. It was an age of emigration and capital expansion, which, together with the rapid and irrevocable changes in the nature of agricultural production, led to the depopulation of local villages and towns and the end of settled communities.

It was also an age of education, which brought a promise of social advancement and a corresponding threat of social dislocation. The Hardy family's increasing financial stability meant that their children could take advantage of a range of local schools. This experience would have profound consequences, however, which Hardy later explored in *Tess of the d'Urbervilles*: *Between the mother, with her fast-perishing lumber of superstitions, folk-lore, dialect, and orally transmitted ballads, and the daughter, with her trained National teachings and Standard knowledge under an infinitely Revised Code, there was a gap of two hundred years as ordinarily understood. When they were together the Jacobean and the Victorian ages were juxtaposed.*[57] Education inevitably divided Hardy from the generation of his parents. His identity was founded in a child's direct and unconscious experience of the sounds and smells of the local district, the quality of the local light, the inflections of local speech, and the habits, customs, stories and songs of his family. He was one of those children who *grow up in solitary country places* and are *imaginative, dreamy, and credulous of vague mysteries*;[58] and everywhere in his writing he explores the character of local knowledge and the romance of traditional culture. *Under the Greenwood Tree*, the novel which deals most closely and nostalgically with the Bockhampton of his childhood, describes how the villagers recognize trees by the sound the wind makes through them and friends by the sound of their footsteps. To *describe* these things is to have lost them: education gave them a name – traditional life-ways – and exiled Hardy from the unconscious experiences of his earliest childhood. He could never feel fully at home in Bockhampton as his parents did.

In 1848 a Church of England 'National School' was set up in the village by Julia Augusta Martin, the wife of the Kingston Maurward landlord, and the Reverend Shirley. Hardy, *thought strong enough to go* to school (until he was five or six, he recalled, *his parents hardly supposed he would survive to grow up*), was among its first pupils.[59] He was already a voracious reader, and marked out as a studious, shy boy (with a big head), who could tackle Dryden's *Virgil* and Johnson's *Rasselas*. He was a great favourite with the patroness: Julia Martin was childless and *had grown passionately fond of Tommy almost from his infancy*.[60] Hardy, too, grew *more attached* to Mrs Martin *than he cared to own*, making her a *lover-like promise of fidelity* when Jemima, angry at the influence the lady of the manor was beginning to exert over her susceptible son, withdrew him from the school in 1849.[61] The latent eroticism of the friendship stayed with Hardy: he remembered years later *the thrilling 'frou-frou' of her four grey silk flounces when she had used to bend over him, and when they brushed against the font as she entered church on Sundays*.[62]

Jemima's decision had consequences: Hardy's father lost the estate building work in retaliation. Luckily, there was plenty of employment available elsewhere in the district; and even more luckily, as a lifeholder, he was independent of the manor, and therefore safe from eviction from his cottage. But in shifting her son from a National School – where 'National' referred to the 'National Society for Promoting the Education of the Poor in the Principles of the Established Church' – to the Nonconformist 'British School' of Isaac Last three miles away in Dorchester, Jemima sent an unambiguous message about her plans for him to the village establishment. It was not that Last was a Dissenter. It was simply thought presumptuous of a 'poor' family like the Hardys to entertain expectations of social advancement through the education of their son. From the first, the joy of learning was, for Hardy, clouded with feelings of social inferiority.

Attendance at Last's school set the pattern of his day-to-day life over the next crucial decade or so of his youth. First, there was the three-mile walk to and from school every day, which accustomed him to the idea of moving freely between the widely different social milieux of village and town. Second, he began to dream of the scholarly life: of perhaps ultimately attending university and taking holy orders. It is unlikely that Hardy shared these secret aspirations with his mother. She encouraged him to take Latin along with the lessons in technical and applied subjects intended to prepare him as a tradesman or professional, but that is probably because she equated learning in the classical languages with social status.

In 1854 Hardy began taking French and continued to read widely in popular classics (Harrison Ainsworth and Dumas). But he could never be among those boys in Dorchester destined for Oxford or Cambridge. On the other side of town, the select pupils taken in by the learned evangelical vicar of Fordington, the Reverend Henry Moule, were reading classics and mathematics, acquiring the knowledge and cultural capital essential for university entry. While still a student of Last's, Hardy was already absorbed in a different kind of scholarly work: the secret labour of self-education. Autodidacticism was something of a craze among aspirational working people in the 1840s and 1850s, and in 1855 and 1856 Hardy purchased the three volumes of that indispensable work of mid-Victorian home-education, Cassell's *Popular Educator*. He was clearly attracted as an adolescent to the idea of a struggle against the odds, and attracted too to the privacy it afforded him: he could make his own mistakes, and reveal himself a learned man when he felt confident enough to do so.

When Hardy was 16 years old his mother's plans for him became clear. He left school and was articled to John Hicks, a Dorchester architect, on 11 July 1856, with a view to being trained in the profession most closely allied with the family business, and therefore most likely to benefit the business by referring work to it. Jemima made all the arrangements. She extracted a substantial discount on the fees *and* committed her (possibly wavering) son to the future she had chosen for him by offering Hicks an advance cash payment in full. Hardy seems, however, to have accepted his destiny with equanimity, perhaps realizing that he would never fulfil his dream of attending university and becoming a don. Yet even the supposedly modest alternative of an architectural career was greeted with scorn among those in Stinsford who believed the sons of bricklayers should know their place. One Sunday at this time Arthur Shirley preached openly in Stinsford church against the insolence of the young upstart with pretensions to a professional career.

There was no such feeling in Hicks's practice, at 39 South Street, Dorchester, where Hardy was given every opportunity to excel, and every opportunity to continue his private studies in classics. Hicks was an easy-going man whose largely ecclesiastical practice flourished for the very same reasons that serious-minded vicars of strong belief like Shirley were given preferment during this period. As the reformist evangelical revival, which had gathered strength in the 1820s, swept through the Church, there arose a demand for the restoration of the many medieval parish church buildings that had fallen into disrepair. Hardy worked on a significant number of these projects (to his later regret: like many

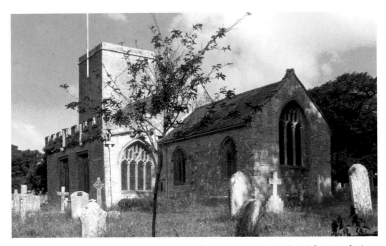

Stinsford Parish Church played a significant part in Hardy's life. His father played in the choir there; the vicar Arthur Shirley once preached against the young Hardy's insolence in seeking a profession career; and after his death his heart was buried in the churchyard.

people he came to see *the craze for indiscriminate church restoration* as a form of fundamentalist vandalism[63]). He was a good draughtsman, and careful in his work, whether it was taking measurements or impressions of decorative capitals, or tracing and copying plans. For the rest of his life he would look back fondly on those days spent drawing in churches and churchyards, memorialized in poems such as 'Copying Architecture in an Old Minster', and in his architectural novel, *A Laodicean* (1881).

Working in the deep shadows of the old village churches dotted around the Dorset countryside encouraged that part of Hardy's nature that was already strongly attracted to the poetic beauty of religious devotion. His still-cherished hopes of a university education, moreover, were focused – as Jude Fawley's were in *Jude the Obscure* – on ordination. At Hicks's, influenced by the evangelical revival, he entered an intensely religious phase which, despite

Henry Robert Bastow in later life.

its low-church temperance, profoundly shaped his life and work. He attended church services regularly, marked personally significant passages in his Bible, began learning Greek, the language of the New Testament, and took his calendar from *The Book of Common Prayer* and Keble's *Christian Year*. Just as the easygoing Anglicanism of Stinsford parish life bred in him a lasting love for the rituals and texts of the Established Church as poetic, not divine, forms of revealed truth, so the fervent evangelicalism of this period outlasted his belief in God, and was transmuted into the great dialectic of suffering and love in his work: the conviction that life, for humans and animals, is a *general drama of pain* and that the best we can hope for is its alleviation by isolated acts of loving-kindness.[64]

Hardy also developed one of those intense adolescent male friendships that thrives on close contact and a shared passion before subsiding quickly. Henry Robert Bastow was a fellow apprentice of Hicks's who was an ardent Baptist. He and Hardy engaged in excited debate about theological and doctrinal points of difference – especially infant versus adult baptism (Bastow had himself been baptised only in 1858). Bastow completed his articles and sailed to Tasmania in 1861, where he worked as an architect and surveyor before settling in Victoria. Once gone, his influence waned. But Bastow left a strong impression: late in life, when Hardy was looking back through the letters in which he was urged on in his spiritual development from remote Tasmania, he wondered what had become of his old fellow apprentice.[65]

The evolutionary theory of Charles Darwin (1809–82) – that species evolved over time through natural selection – was based on his observations of wildlife and fossils on a five-year voyage around the world aboard HMS *Beagle* in the 1830s. On the voyage Darwin read and was influenced by Charles Lyell's *Principles of Geology* (1830), which argued that geological processes shaped landforms over aeons. Gideon Algernon Mantell, author of *The Wonders of Geology*, was ridiculed for deducing, rightly, that the fossil animals he had discovered were from the Mesozoic era – dinosaurs.

The fervent Bastow was not Hardy's only intimate friend during this period. In 1857, when he was 17, he began a close friendship with Horace Moule, the 25-year-old fourth son of the vicar of Fordington. A more different man from Bastow could hardly be imagined. Moule was handsome, charming, well educated, and already widely published. He had studied at Oxford and Cambridge and regularly wrote reviews for the leading quarterly periodicals. While Hardy was grappling with the Greek New Testament and responding to Bastow's spiritual advice and encouragement, he was also therefore being introduced to a glamorous new world of progressive scholarship and religious controversy. In 1858, on the eve of the publication of Darwin's explosive *On the Origin of Species* (1859), Moule lent Hardy his copy of Gideon Algernon Mantell's *The Wonders of Geology* – a dangerous book for the son of a devout and learned evangelical vicar, as Angel Clare discovers in *Tess of the d'Urbervilles*.[66] This friendship also drew Hardy into the 'great Victorian drama of unbelief', the culture of honest doubt that 'forced [the Victorians], against their deepest longings, to abandon the faith'.[67] It would shape his moral, philosophical and artistic outlook, as he, too, struggled to find a credible source of spiritual authority to replace untenable religious worldviews and social and cultural traditions under assault from industrialization and rapid urban population growth.

Hardy idolized Moule. For all his gifts and promise, however, he suffered from clinical depression and was sliding into alcoholism when his impressionable protégé came to know him. A man of advanced opinions, Moule was tormented by frequent ideological conflict with his father, who was an important theologian and thinker in his own right. He was never able to complete his degrees at Oxford or Cambridge, and often struggled to finish the reviewing work he took on for *Blackwood's* or *Fraser's*. In despair he helped out with some of his father's pupils and made himself available as a coach to young middle-class Dorset men who aspired to enter Oxford or Cambridge when the new middle-class competitive examination entry system was set up in 1858. In 1860, he went missing on binges in Salisbury, and again in Paris, when preparing pupils for the exams.

Destined for a professional career, Hardy could never hope to be one of Moule's paying pupils, and there is little evidence that his friend ever encouraged him to pursue his dream beyond the study of Latin and Greek. And he seems not, on the face of it, to have been a very promising scholar, unlike Moule's dazzling protégé Hooper Tolbort, whose remarkable story reads like a fable of mid-Victorian self-helpfulness. Tolbort, the son of an ironmonger, was

The Reverend Henry Moule and family outside Fordington Vicarage. Horace Moule is standing fifth from the right.

given enough freedom and leisure to cultivate his prodigious talent and almost monomaniacal powers of concentration. An extraordinary polymath with a gift for languages, Tolbort was educated by the Reverend William Barnes, the renowned Dorset dialect poet and philologist (whose school was next-door to Hicks's office: Hardy and Bastow would occasionally ask Barnes to adjudicate a grammatical dispute). Tolbort earned first place in the Oxford middle-class examinations, repeated his success in the Indian Civil Service Examination, and won a post in India, where he contracted consumption in the early 1880s.

Hardy got to know Tolbort well, and soon came to the realization – perhaps reminded of George Eliot's Casaubon in *Middlemarch* – that there was after all something uncongenial and slightly irksome about a scholar's life. Tolbort's genius, he later wrote in his obituary in the *Dorset County Chronicle*, was *receptive rather than productive*, repeating almost verbatim the characteristic he had explored in the early 1870s in Stephen Smith, the hero of *A Pair of Blue Eyes*, who is a curious composite portrait of elements of Tolbort and Hardy. Stephen belonged to a type Hardy believed was becoming more numerous as the nation *gets older, individuality fades, and education spreads; that is, his brain had extraordinary receptive powers, and not an atom of creativeness. Quickly acquiring any kind of knowledge he saw around him ... he changed colour like a chameleon as the society he found himself in assumed a higher and more artificial tone. He had not an original idea, and yet there was scarcely an idea to which, under proper training, he could not have added a respectable co-ordinate.*[68]

Hardy also began to feel deeply the limitations of his life as a provincial architect, copying, taking measurements and numbering stones. He must have felt, too, watching Hicks at work, that even fully qualified he might never be able to do what his father did every day of his life: actually *make* something – originate something. He laboured away at his classics studies in the mornings before work and during quiet times at the office, struggling against a mind too wayward and imaginative for the drudgery of scholarship. He was already thinking of moving to London, and he was already writing poetry.

# Professional 1862–8

On 17 April 1862, the 21-year-old Hardy, looking a bit like *a chappie with no chin, and a moustache like a lady's eyebrow*,[69] bought himself a train ticket to London – a return, just in case things didn't go well. Who can say how many others just like him arrived from the countryside that day, and what their fate was? More than half the male population of London in 1862 had been born elsewhere,[70] and ominously for Hardy, almost the first person he met in the capital warned him that he probably wouldn't last: *'Wait till you have walked the streets a few weeks', he said satirically, 'and your elbows begin to shine, and the hems of your trousers get frayed, as if nibbled by rats! Only practical men are wanted here'.* But Hardy had inherited his mother's sharp realism and good sense, and he soon settled down to the business of getting ahead in his profession. Over the next five years, the most vital in his formation as a writer, he would abandon, successively, the dreams and schemes of a scholar's life, a clergyman's life, a poet's life, and – finally – an architect's life. Hardy continued to study extremely hard under his own, and to a lessening degree Moule's, direction. He typically spent many hours each night, from the evening until midnight, at his books, but gradually gave up the laborious translation work in the classics (essential for university entry) and began to concentrate instead on other things: pre-eminently reading and learning the craft of poetry. Exposed to advanced metropolitan ideas and culture, the pervasive atmosphere of religious doubt

Thomas Hardy, aged 19.

among liberals, the emerging ethos of professionalism, and the sheer necessity of surviving daily life in a big city, he would return to Bockhampton a changed man.

He arrived in *the London of Dickens and Thackeray*, Hardy later recalled: a London almost unrecognizable to later generations.[71] Until the end of his life, he would look back fondly on nights spent dancing at Willis's Rooms, Cremorne Gardens, and elsewhere: venues with all the seedy Regency allure of the Vauxhall Gardens in Thackeray's *Vanity Fair* (1849). He also attended one of Dickens's celebrated public readings, just when *Our Mutual Friend* (appearing, in monthly instalments in 1864–5) was re-drawing the imagined city of *Oliver Twist* (1838) and *Bleak House* (1853) with the Thames at its heart: a city accumulating money and filth. All this immense wealth and decay was the subject of a vast discourse of social investigation at this time. The utilitarian character of mid-Victorian government, supported by a new pros-perity and stability, responded to the rapid expansion of the cities by gathering statistics, undertaking sociological studies, commis-sioning boards of inquiry, and bringing down Acts of Parliament. All of this reformist activity led to a massive investment of capital and labour in urban infrastructure improvement during the period of Hardy's first stay.

As a result, the London of Dickens and Thackeray was disap-pearing before his eyes. Writing for a post-Great-War readership in the *Life*, he emphasizes the old. *Hungerford Market was still in being where the Charing Cross Station now stands*, he recalls, and there was *no Thames Embankment. Temple Bar still stood in its place, and the huge block of buildings known as the Law Courts was not erected. Holborn Hill was still a steep and noisy thoroughfare which almost broke the legs of the slipping horses ... There was no underground railway.*[72] All that is true; but Hardy did watch the Thames Embankment being built (1862–74), and the new bridges (Westminster Bridge and Charing Cross Bridge in 1862) reaching across the river. He witnessed the achievements of the first phase of the legendary Metropolitan Board of Works (empowered by the 1855 Metropolis Manage-ment Act), which built street pavements, brought in piped water and gas, and completely overhauled the city's sewage and drainage system. The Metropolitan Line, the first in the London Under-ground, was opened in 1863, supplementing the services of the vast and still-expanding overground railway system.

Public works on such a massive scale needed a ready supply of planners and architects, so Hardy's arrival in London was timely.

It was also to his advantage that the steady demand for church restoration which supported Hicks in Dorchester was even greater in London. Hardy secured a place almost immediately as an assistant in the office of Arthur Blomfield, the 33-year-old son of Charles James Blomfield, the former Bishop of London who had overseen the building of hundreds of new churches in the capital in the first half of the 19th century. Blomfield's premises were situated (after 1863) off the Strand on Adelphi Terrace overlooking the Thames. Blomfield had built up a successful practice working in the period's dominant style, Gothic, and was seeking *a young Gothic draughtsman who could restore and design churches and rectory-houses.*[73] Hardy's experience with Hicks proved ideal. Blomfield was an easy-going employer, fondly remembered for his good humour and the prankish bonhomie of his office. Blomfield *and his pupils, including Hardy, used to get on with their architecture ... by singing glees and catches at intervals during office hours.*[74] Noticing his new junior's musical talent, Blomfield invited him to join the office choir. Hardy recalled, too, the high-jinks of Blomfield's young *Tory and Churchy* pupils, who got into trouble for dropping bits of paper on the heads of members of the ultra-radical Reform League, which had offices on the floor below.[75]

Blomfield soon came to trust Hardy professionally, too, offering him other jobs and responsibilities on top of his architectural drawing work. When the firm was commissioned to supervise *the carrying of a cutting by the Midland Railway through Old St. Pancras Churchyard, which would necessitate the removal of many hundreds of coffins, and bones in huge quantities,*[76] he deputed Hardy to oversee the clerk-of-works. Every evening on his way home to 16 Westbourne Park Villas, where he lived for most of his first London stay, Hardy stopped at St Pancras to ensure that *new coffins* were *being provided for those that came apart in lifting, and for loose skeletons.*[77] These added duties encouraged the young architect to advance himself in his profession. He was elected to the Architectural

View from my window
16. 1P. P. V.
June 22-66.
[*] part 8 in evening.

Hardy's sketch of the view from his window at 16 Westbourne Park Villas.

Association, and entered the requisite competitions (in 1863 his essay 'On the Application of Coloured Bricks and Terracotta to Modern Architecture' won the silver medal in a Royal Institute of British Architects competition). He spent his spare time making sketches and notes from buildings, and prepared for the RIBA voluntary examinations.

But at some point in the 1860s, it became clear to him that architecture could never satisfy him creatively. He was diligent and self-educated, but he learned that the architect 'more than any other artist' would be 'at the mercy of his personal employer'.[78] For a lowly assistant like Hardy, moreover, there was no opportunity for creativity of any kind: *architectural drawing in which the actual designing had no great part was monotonous and mechanical.*[79]

The Midland Railway Hotel at the front of St Pancras Station. While working for the architect Arthur Blomfield in London in the early 1860s, Hardy supervised the construction of a railway cutting through Old St Pancras Churchyard during the building of the station.

More significantly, he realized that he had *little inclination*, or ready capital, *for getting into social affairs and influential sets which would help him start a practice of his own.*[80] Architecture offered some degree of social mobility, but not without prodigious talent, careful cultivation of patrons and single-minded dedication.[81]

Hardy's literary aspirations remained uppermost, in any case, and the building boom allowed him to pursue them comfortably enough. In 1865, a notebook entry reveals him thinking of *cutting Arch$^e$ if success* in literature. But then, as if remembering his real situation, he reassuringly scribbles on the endpaper of the notebook: – *If lit. fails, try Arch.*[82] Horace Moule suggested he try getting a job writing 'a column of condensed London news & talk' for a country newspaper.[83] At about this time it also occurred to him that he might merge the two *by becoming an art-critic for the* *press, particularly in the province of architectural art.*[84] In this vein, his first published piece, a light-hearted sketch in *Chambers's Journal* entitled 'How I Built Myself a House', nicely combined his professional and recreational interests.[85]

And Hardy soon found that he didn't need to find a new job to combine literature and architecture. The free and easy atmosphere of Blomfield's practice encouraged him, and he *used to deliver short … talks on poets and poetry to … pupils and assistants on afternoons when there was not much to be done, or at all events when not much was done.*[86] Having once abandoned any thought of taking architecture further, he found the ways and means of supporting his writing until he could establish himself in some way in literature. Over the coming years he would have the liberty of taking up architectural jobs as his basic needs dictated, and slipping away again when he had saved enough money to support himself through a period of writing.

London, meanwhile, was a treasure-house for a young provincial man of eclectic tastes and intellectual curiosity, passionate about ideas and politics, art, literature, theatre and music. With characteristic application, Hardy spent 20 minutes each lunchtime at the National Gallery, restricting himself to studying just one picture each day. The progress of his practical studies in art appreciation (apparently aided by a guidebook) was meticulously recorded in an 1863 notebook he entitled 'Schools of Painting'. It contains brief *aides-memoires* on the work of major painters from the early Renaissance through to the age of Constable. There is nothing in the notebook to suggest that Hardy was forming his own tastes, or to indicate the real significance of these visits to the development of his own art. The entries reflect the mind of a would-be connoisseur, not a would-be poet with an intensely visual imagination. Yet these visits would prove vital to Hardy's writing.[87] Already in 1865 he notes down in another diary: *The form on the canvas which immortalizes the painter is but the last of a series of tentative*

*and abandoned sketches each of which probably contained some particular
feature nearer perfection than any part of the finished product.*[88]

Hardy was also an avid theatre- and opera-goer, and his close
familiarity with the London stage in the 1860s – from the classical
repertoire to popular comedies, pantomimes and melodramas –
undoubtedly contributed to the pronounced theatricality of his
writing. He was, in particular, deeply influenced by Shakespeare
at this time. He bought a ten-volume edition of the *Complete Works*
in 1863, and the heavy underlinings and marginal annotations
confirm that he read Shakespeare *more closely from 23 to 26* than at any
other time of his life.[89] He saw Charles Kean and his wife perform
their famous Shakespearean roles at the Princess's Theatre, and Mrs
Scott-Siddons at the Haymarket. He and a fellow-worker from
Blomfield's attended the whole of Samuel Phelps's Shakespeare
series at Drury Lane, propping their editions of the plays up against
the pit barrier – *a severe enough test for the actors if they noticed the two
enthusiasts.*[90] He also went to Covent Garden and Her Majesty's
two or three times a week, where he developed a great love for the
popular Italian operas of the day, by Rossini, Bellini, Donizetti and
Verdi, and closely followed the careers of the leading singers.

Naturally it occurred to Hardy that there might be a future
writing for the stage. Playwrights were not well remunerated at
this time, however (the royalty payment system was not introduced until the end of the decade, and writers only began to
benefit substantially in the 1880s); and Hardy's idea of writing
blank verse dramas – his particular form of the 'Shakespearian
longings' that afflicted all the Victorians, as V S Pritchett once
observed[91] – would scarcely have guaranteed him an income. Eager
to school himself in the technicalities of the stage, he took parts as
a *nondescript* in the pantomime of the 'Forty Thieves' on the Covent
Garden stage and *in a representation of the Oxford and Cambridge
boat-race*. It was a sobering experience: *almost the first moment of his
sight of stage realities disinclined him to push further in that direction.*[92]

Impressed, surely, by the tremendous richness and inventiveness of Shakespeare's language, Hardy began to teach himself the craft of poetry through a long and idiosyncratic labour of linguistic imitation and exercise. His chief primers were Palgrave's *Golden Treasury* (a gift from Moule in 1862), Nuttall's *Standard Pronouncing Dictionary* and Walker's *Rhyming Dictionary*, an introductory English literary history, standard volumes of the English poets, including Spenser, Milton, Dryden, Wordsworth, Coleridge and Shelley, the just-published *Poems and Ballads* of Swinburne (1866) and the ten-volume Shakespeare. He began a new notebook, curiously entitled 'Studies, Specimens &c', in the manner of an amateur natural historian. His aim in starting the notebook seems to have been to progress beyond stylistic imitation to his own poetic voice as quickly as possible. The technique he used, reminiscent of the warm-up games played in creative writing classes now, was to ignore the prosodic structure and speech cadences of the poetic line altogether. Instead he tried generating poetry out of the forced juxtaposition of isolated words and phrases. In this way, presumably, Hardy meant to teach himself to think metaphorically: to throw off stale habits of thought and speech, and see the world afresh through the power of linguistic re-association. In many examples, the energy of these exercises is openly erotic. Using a plain sequence of words from the dictionary, for instance, he extemporizes: *the / biting want : catch of lip by lip : long / kisses & short ceasings: sweet chafe / of ..: chills : close circuits of me.*[93]

Algernon Charles Swinburne (1837–1909) wrote poetry of dazzling metrical variety which, despite its antique costume of (mostly) Greek paganism, was ultra-radical in its politics and scandalous in its social and sexual forthrightness, earning Morley's sobriquet 'the libidinous laureate of a pack of satyrs'. Like Hardy, Swinburne was deeply influenced by Shelley's radicalism. In 1905 he reported to Hardy the words of an unnamed critic: 'Swinburne planteth, Hardy watereth, and Satan giveth the increase'.

Little or none of that eroticism emerges, explicitly at least, in the poems preserved by Hardy from this period, all of which were composed alongside these stylistic experiments. They show the young poet striving to invest standard forms (most notably the sonnet) with verbal, syntactical, rhythmic and narrative innovation. Not surprisingly, they were all rejected by magazine editors in the 1860s – readers and critics were still puzzled by them when the poems finally appeared 30 years later – no doubt because of their seeming ineptitude and lack of fluency and musicality. They also deal very frankly with the failure of sexual relationships, which could hardly have helped. George Meredith's candid, groundbreaking treatment of the same themes in 'Modern Love' (1862), parts of which had appeared in the magazine *Once a Week*, might have convinced Hardy that the time was right. But when it was published as a volume, *Modern Love and Other Poems* was vehemently attacked for its vulgarity, cynicism, and obscurity.[94] Hardy wrote his own long sonnet sequence of *love's decline* in the manner of 'Modern Love' in 1866, the 'She, to Him' sonnets (of which he retained only four for later publication).[95] Like Meredith's poem, it had its roots in Hardy's personal life.

For most of his time in London, between 1863 and 1867, he was involved in a relationship with Eliza Bright Nicholls, a devout young woman who had grown up on the Dorset coast (her father was the coastguard at Kimmeridge Bay) and who worked as a lady's maid in a house close by Westbourne Park Villas until 1865. Little is known of the relationship, although there is evidence that the couple became engaged – certainly the pious and earnest Eliza believed them to be. Soon, though, Hardy cooled, and when Eliza's work took her away from London he began to lose interest, momentarily shifting his attention to her sister, before the relationship finally collapsed. The 'She, to Him' sonnets suggest that the end of the affair was protracted and extremely painful on both sides. The best of the early London poems, 'Neutral Tones' (1867), transmutes the experience into a nightmarish vision of loss:

> *We stood by a pond that winter day,*
> *And the sun was white, as though chidden of God,*
> *And a few leaves lay on the starving sod;*
> *   – They had fallen from an ash, and were gray.*

> *Your eyes on me were as eyes that rove*
> *Over tedious riddles solved years ago;*
> *And some words played between us to and fro*
> *   On which lost the more by our love.*

> *The smile on your mouth was the deadest thing*
> *Alive enough to have strength to die;*
> *And a grin of bitterness swept thereby*
> *   Like an ominous bird a-wing ...*

> *Since then, keen lessons that love deceives,*
> *And wrings with wrong, have shaped to me*
> *Your face, and the God-curst sun, and a tree,*
> *   And a pond edged with grayish leaves.*[96]

As the blighted landscape with its *God-curst sun* suggests, here and in other early lyrics a sexual crisis is mixed up with a religious crisis. One poem, in fact, goes much further, imagining a world where we might actually *long* for God's curse, as the speaker in 'Hap' (1866) does, wishing that some immortal being somewhere would take pleasure in his pain and suffering. *But not so.* There is no such being: all that exists is *Crass Casualty*, which would have *as readily strown / Blisses about my pilgrimage as pain.*[97] Hardy was preoccupied with *Nature's Indifference* from his beginnings as a poet, then, so he must have realized almost immediately the absurdity of his idea of *combining poetry and the Church* in mid-1865 by taking a degree at University and applying for a curacy in a country village.[98] He already knew by then, as the anguished Jude the Obscure does not at first, that his idealization of the religious life was, deep down, an idealization of gentility and a fantasy of the cosseted intellectual life. Pencilled into the margin of his Bible with the date 11 September 1864 (and later erased), was that iconic mid-Victorian word: *doubt.*

Hardy had already read *On the Origin of Species* and through Moule had access to the controversial rationalist literature of the period: the liberal scientific and philosophical challenges to religious certainty. He read Herbert Spencer who, under the influence of Auguste Comte's post-Christian world-system, positivism, devoted his life to expanding Darwin's evolutionary ideas into a total theory of psychological, social and cultural organization and behaviour. In the same vein, Hardy made detailed drawings based on the theories of the passions formulated by the French Utopian socialist, Fourier. He had also read the explosive 1860 *Essays and Reviews*, by the so-called 'Seven Against Christ', before he came to London, and was therefore familiar with the latest heretical geological and biological theories, and with the tradition of the Higher Criticism. Yet his crisis – if that is what it was: perhaps turning-point is more accurate – seems to have occurred in 1865 when he was reading the seminal work of the most profound Christian apologist of his generation, John Henry Newman's *Apologia Pro Vita Sua*.[99] Later he condescendingly dismissed *Poor Newman!* whose *gentle childish faith in revelation and tradition must have made him a very charming character.*[100] Yet Hardy's surviving notebooks show detailed excerpts from only one book for this London period, the *Apologia*. How well he must have recognized himself in Newman. In July 1865 his diary records: *Sunday. To Westminster Abbey morning service. Stayed to the sacrament. A very odd experience, amid a crowd of strangers.*[101] Hardy feared, as Newman did, the loss of *a great truth for the memory*, a *common history, common memories, and intercourse of mind with mind in the past*.[102] It was at this time that he began to *practise orthodoxy*: to attend church for the sake of old associations, cherishing its rituals as an aesthetic and a personal experience – as a poetry.[103]

A brief remark from the *Apologia* which Hardy copied down in 1865 evokes better than anything else the allure that the world of mid-Victorian politics and thought must have held for a young man with progressive ideas and literary ambitions. 'The truth was', Newman confessed, 'I was beginning to prefer intellectual excellence to moral: I was drifting in the direction of liberalism.'[104] The few years of Hardy's first London stay were years of remarkable political changes, and Hardy was swept up in them. In October 1865, he attended the Westminster Abbey funeral of the Prime Minister, Lord Palmerston, who had, with W E Gladstone, laid the foundations for the modern Liberal party. Gladstone himself formed the first Liberal government in 1868, elected because it brought together a powerful alliance of elitist Whig progressivists, populist *laissez-faire* and free-trade ideologies (which united the interests of the Nonconformist industrial north and rural small businesses like the Hardys'), and the 'respectable' urban working classes, newly enfranchised by the 1867 Reform Act. Ideologically, liberalism placed its emphasis on the primacy of the rights and freedoms of individuals in their relations with the state and its political institutions, freedom of religious expression and freedom before the law, the sanctity of private property, and intellectual and artistic freedom.

Hardy and his friends knew John Stuart Mill's *On Liberty* (1867), the bible of liberalism, *almost by heart* in those years;[105] and he had vivid memories of seeing Mill on the hustings in Covent Garden in 1865. What he remembered most clearly of that spectacle, he later wrote, was the image of *a man out of place*: a man too learned to make himself comprehensible to the crowd he was vainly trying to persuade. *He stood bareheaded, and his vast pale brow, so thin-skinned as to show the blue veins, sloped back like a stretching upland, and conveyed to the observer a curious sense of perilous exposure.*[106] That image made a lasting impression on Hardy, who was himself being formed as a liberal intellectual in literary London. It wasn't the London of Dickens and Thackeray any more in that sense, either. It was the London of the liberals – Meredith and Leslie Stephen (both of them soon to be important figures for Hardy); and Matthew Arnold, George Eliot and Anthony Trollope (whose Barchester was an important precursor for Wessex). Hardy never mixed himself up in politics, believing that public life was out of his sphere and that social change could just as effectively be brought about by the free thought and discussion which art encouraged. And truly, the great liberal issues of the mid-century were the great issues of his fiction: the meaning of individual freedom, the role of culture, the subjection of women.

In 1868, Hardy listed Mill's essay 'On Individuality' (a chapter of *On Liberty*) among his *cures for despair*, hinting in the *Life* that he had just emerged from *a time of mental depression over his work and prospects*.[107] That time seems to have begun in the early summer of 1867, when he fell suddenly and unaccountably ill in London. Over the late spring months he grew increasingly pallid and lethargic until *he had scarcely physical power left him to hold the pencil and square*.[108] At first he put the cause down to the Dickensian oppressiveness of the city he loved, with its teeming populace, thick polluted air, and streets full of refuse and excrement. Most of all he recoiled from the stench of the Thames running alongside Adelphi Terrace, which rose fetid into the air at low tide on hot days. But there was more to it than that. Hardy was worn out from years of studying by lamplight night after night in his West-bourne Park rooms. That labour had brought him little or no reward as yet – only unfinished translations, unpublished poems and unrealistic expectations – and it seems that his enervation was a symptom of real mental depression. Trapped in the drudgery of architectural work, and the imperative of trying to get ahead, to do something with himself and make something *of* himself, he fell into *the fitful yet mechanical and monotonous existence that befalls many a young man in London lodgings*.[109] On his 25th birthday, 2 June 1865, he reflected morosely that he felt as if he *had lived a long time, and done very little*.[110] But he *constitutionally shrank from the business of social advancement, caring for life as an emotion rather than … a science of climbing, in which respect he was quizzed by his acquaintance for his lack of ambition*.[111] There is no saying how much of himself he had to suppress – his West Country accent and humble origins, his unrealized hopes and failed love affairs, his dissatisfaction with the tedium of the office, his feelings of inadequacy and loneliness – just to survive.

Hardy must have remembered with some bitterness the cynical advice he had received on his first day in London: *Only practical men are wanted here.* He felt he could only be restored to health by returning home. Luckily, his old employer John Hicks was laid up with gout and looking for an assistant to help with church restoration work. Hardy left London in July 1867, and, although he quickly fell into his old way of life, sleeping in the Bockhampton cottage and walking the three miles into Dorchester each day, he came back *with very different ideas of things*.[112] London had not just made him an architect; it had made him a professional. Discontented, he would never return to full-time architecture, preferring short stints and refusing all offers of permanent work. Yet he was always in demand, his work was always valued, and even brief professional connections became longstanding friendships. Ironically, then, he suddenly *became more practical*[113] in Bockhampton – partly, no doubt, because he was back in his mother's house; but partly, too, because he was beginning to think about literature as a profession rather than a calling. He finally admitted the worst to himself: that 'the poor poet has not in these days, nor has had for two hundred years, a dog's chance' (in the words of Sir Arthur Quiller-Couch, later a friend).[114] Poetry was, he resolved, *a waste of labour*.[115] He needed a *clear call ... which course in life to take – the course he loved, and which was his natural instinct, that of letters, or the course all practical wisdom dictated – that of architecture*.[116] At last he succumbed to the inevitable, and began to think about writing prose fiction for the popular market.

Hardy's tentativeness was understandable. To him, poetry was *the essence of all imaginative and emotional literature*,[117] whereas the status of the novel was still uncertain, despite the towering achievements of Dickens, Thackeray and, latterly, George Eliot. The commercial fiction market was booming in the 1860s, and demand for serialized novels by the many new magazines put intense pressure on authors to produce stories reflecting the mainstream values of hard work, thrift, self-determination and homely femininity. One response to this was a sedate domestic realism; another was the more interesting and daring sensation novel which began with Wilkie Collins and Dickens, and soon spread through the serial markets, where it was dominated by the work of Mary Elizabeth Braddon and Ellen Wood.

Thinking of Thackeray's mordant social satire *Vanity Fair*, Hardy viewed *novel writing of the highest kind as a perfect and truthful representation of actual life*, and believed that the best novels *have anything but an elevating tendency, and on that account are particularly unfitted for young people – from their very truthfulness* (he is instructing his sister in literary appreciation in 1863 here; three decades later he would defend the truthfulness of his own work against accusations of its unfitness for young readers).[118] On the model of *Vanity Fair* ('A Novel Without a Hero'), and armed with his Shelley and Mill's *On Liberty*, he began one of his own: *The Poor Man and the Lady. / A Story with no plot; / Containing some original verses* (he quickly saw that the hybrid form would be unlikely to attract a publisher, and absorbed the verses into the prose). Coming back to Bockhampton must have revived memories of the youthful passions he had left behind when he went to London, for they form the basis of the story, or what is known of it: that of the difficulties and ultimate failure of love relationships between the classes. Dealing with the prohibited love of an impoverished young architect for a woman of the local gentry, its biographical origins may lie in his mutual infatuation with Julia Augusta Martin of Kingston Maurward, fresh in his mind from an awkward visit he had paid her in London; and in an old impossible love for Louisa Harding, the daughter of a local farmer whom Hardy could only admire from afar. But biographical explanations of this kind are inadequate, for this is the *key* plot of Hardy's fiction, repeated in many variations throughout the next three decades.

The sensation novel updated many of the elements of the Gothic thriller – endangered heroines, treacherous foreigners, imprisonment, mistaken identity, bigamy – by placing them in an ordinary modern-day setting, exploiting new technologies (the railway) and ways of life, and infusing them with the dialogue and plot conventions of stage melodrama. The most famous examples of the genre are Wilkie Collins's *The Woman in White* (1859), Mrs Henry Wood's *East Lynne* (1861) and Mary Elizabeth Braddon's *Lady Audley's Secret* (1862).

It allows him to explore imaginatively the real possibilities and limits of the much vaunted social meritocracy in mid-Victorian Britain – the guarantee of personal advancement based on hard work which had thrust him into professional life. In this plot physical desire and material ambition coalesce or collide in complicated romantic entanglements which promise upward social mobility for one partner and threaten social regression for the other; and, as the plot makes clear, these conditions affect men and women differently.

By early 1868, Hardy had started on the fair copy of *The Poor Man*. In between working for Hicks he finished the manuscript and sent it off to Alexander Macmillan (on Horace Moule's advice) on 25 July 1868. When a letter came back a fortnight later he was relieved to learn that his *haphazard attempt at fiction* had been well received.[119] Macmillan wrote a long letter explaining what was wrong with the novel and why he could not publish it – though others might, he readily allowed. Encouraged, Hardy sent the manuscript off to Chapman and Hall, the publishers of Dickens, who finally agreed to publish *The Poor Man* if Hardy would put up £20 of his own. He did, and waited for the proofs to arrive. Instead, a note came asking him to meet with the publisher's reader in London: the novelist George Meredith.

Hardy recalled how Meredith, manuscript in hand, counselled him in the strongest terms against publishing the novel. *The Poor Man* was, as Hardy later described it, an inflammatory *dramatic satire of the squirearchy and nobility, London society, the vulgarity of the middle class, modern Christianity, church restoration, and political and domestic morals in general*.[120] Meredith felt that if the young author *wished to do anything practical at literature*, he really ought not to set out by taking angry swipes at so many of his readers or by declaring himself a *socialistic, not to say revolutionary* writer – which he wasn't, as Meredith well recognized.[121] The appeal to practicality found its mark.

# Novelist 1868–82

It wasn't the clear call Hardy had been waiting for, but he was elated. Two leading publishers and two eminent literary men had been sufficiently impressed by *The Poor Man* to respond at length and with warm encouragement: 'If the man is young, there is stuff and promise in him', John Morley, Macmillan's reader, declared in his report.[122] But Hardy was already 29 years old. It was 13 years since he had begun as Hicks's pupil. Despite everything – the grinding self-education, the years in London, the dozens of poems, and now the completed novel – he was still, in the eyes of the world, and especially the close world of Bockhampton and Dorchester, a lowly architect's assistant. Frustrated and in a hurry, he was determined to find out what publishers wanted. He wrote to Macmillan asking him to suggest the sort of story he might do best. In response to Morley's praise he began a novel entirely *of rural scenes & humble life*,[123] but set it aside to follow Meredith's advice: *a novel with a purely artistic purpose* (as distinct from a polemical purpose) and *a more complicated 'plot'*.[124] The result was *Desperate Remedies*.

Meanwhile, events in Dorchester had taken an unexpected turn. In February 1869 Hicks, who was only 54, died suddenly. His practice was sold to a Weymouth architect, G R Crickmay, who had no experience with Gothic and so asked Hardy to stay on and help him finish Hicks's outstanding church restoration projects. Hardy was assigned the rebuilding of Turnworth Church – by far his biggest architectural undertaking. For most of the rest of the

Tryphena Sparks, Hardy's cousin.

year he lived and worked in Weymouth, seeing through this and other jobs, and in his spare time swimming and dancing, going home at weekends, and getting on with *Desperate Remedies*. Early in 1870, he decided to decamp to the winter quiet of the Bockhampton cottage to finish his novel away from distractions. That was now possible because his much younger Puddletown cousin, Tryphena Sparks, of whom he had been seeing a great deal over the previous two years, had taken herself off to London to begin training as a teacher. She was pretty, vivacious, intelligent and, like Hardy, upwardly mobile (she became headmistress of a school in Plymouth, and eventually married a well-heeled publican). Hardy had been attracted to her, as he had been to her older sister Martha years earlier, and was much in the company of her family, with whom he had always been on close terms. Only afterwards, evidently, did he realize that he had been in love with Tryphena;

but it was all too late by then. A poem in his first collection, *Wessex Poems* (1898), commemorates her – she died in early middle age in 1890 – and expresses those regrets, calling her his *lost prize* and looking back to the days *when her dreams were upbrimming with light, / And with laughter her eyes*.[125]

In February, Crickmay contacted Hardy about the one Hicks commission still outstanding: the rebuilding of the dilapidated medieval parish church of St Juliot in north Cornwall, a project which had been languishing for nearly two years. Hardy agreed, but asked to put it off until he had finished *Desperate Remedies*. A month or so later, he sent the manuscript to Macmillan, and on Monday 7 March 1870 set off on the long journey west in the starlight of early morning. St Juliot was only a hundred miles from Bockhampton, but it was an isolated hamlet on a remote and inhospitable part of the coast 'where newspapers rarely penetrated, ... [and] where new books rarely came, or strangers'.[126] The route involved 'changing trains many times, and waiting at stations',[127] and when Hardy reached Launceston late in the afternoon, he still had 16 miles to go by horse-drawn carriage or cart. Night had fallen by the time he finally arrived at the rectory, where he was surprised to find neither the rector, Cadell Holder, nor his wife, Helen, there to greet him. She was nursing her husband upstairs (he was laid up with gout) and had asked her sister, Emma Lavinia Gifford, to settle the visiting architect in. Emma had accompanied the newlyweds to the rectory in 1868, partly to escape her father, a Plymouth solicitor given to spasmodic outbreaks of drunkenness, and partly to be a companion for Helen, who was 35 years younger than her new husband. In doing so Emma must have resigned herself to the unpleasant prospect of spinsterhood – she was, like Hardy, nearly 30 – or at the very least to marrying well below her social class. The niece of a Canon in the Church of England who later became Archdeacon of London, she had social pretensions, and found little in St Juliot besides 'a cold, often ill-natured, working class'.[128]

Yet the extreme remoteness and wildness of the place, and the very improbability of attracting a genteel suitor out there, also encouraged in Emma a sense of freedom from social constraint which few women in her social position, or with her airs, might have been expected to enjoy. She was captivated by the romantic landscape and its Arthurian associations: not just Tintagel Castle but the whole 'beautiful sea-coast, and the wild Atlantic Ocean rolling in with its magnificent waves and spray, its white gulls, and black choughs and grey puffins, its cliffs and rocks and gorgeous sunsettings'.[129] Dressed eccentrically in a long brown habit and a brown hat over her corn-coloured hair, she looked every bit the romantic heroine haunting the landscape on her brown mare Fanny. She rode freely and often recklessly about the neighbour- hood, 'scampering up and down the hills ... alone, wanting no protection, the rain going down my back often, and my hair floating on the wind'.[130]

The rectory was nestled into a hillside and overlooked its own extensive and sheltered gardens, surrounding farmlands and the descending belt of deep woodland that followed the nearby Valency river down the valley to the sea. This placid outlook would have given the arriving Hardy little sense of the rugged, windswept open country of the cliff-tops high above Pentargan Bay only a mile or so away. Nor could he have guessed how, within the week, he would have fallen in love with *the opal and the sapphire of that wandering western sea, / And the woman riding high above with bright hair flapping free*.[131] He quickly completed the formal business of the trip, making initial drawings and measurements of the decrepit church with his measuring-tape and rule, and spent the rest of the week in Emma's company. They talked eagerly about literature (she noticed a piece of blue paper sticking out of his pocket when he arrived: it was a poem), played music and sang in the evenings, met local friends, and went out riding and walking. Hardy left on Friday, but returned in the summer for a three-week holiday, when the courtship flourished. Riding Fanny, and with Hardy walking by her side, Emma 'showed him some ... of the neighbourhood – the cliffs, along the roads, and through the scattered hamlets ... to Tintagel and Trebarwith Strand ...[and] other places on the coast'.[132] The couple followed the Valency down the *leafed alley*[133] to Boscastle, picnicking along the way and losing a crystal tumbler in a waterfall. They went out sketching together, or sat in a high secluded spot in the garden overlooking the valley. By the time he returned to Bockhampton he was, informally at any rate, engaged to be married. A few sentences from their only surviving love letter, written by Emma in October 1870 (she later burned the rest: this one escaped only because Hardy transcribed it and absorbed it into Chapter 19 of *A Pair of Blue Eyes*), is wonderfully redolent of the visionary atmosphere and erotic feeling Hardy always associated with this brief, intense time: '... This dream of my life – no, not dream, for what is actually going on around me seems a dream rather... . I take him (the reserved man) as I do the Bible; find out what I can, compare one text with another, & believe the rest in a lump of simple faith'.[134] From this it would appear that the shy, unhandsome 'reserved' Hardy succeeded in wooing Emma in his letters – the 'texts' she compares are presumably the lover on paper and the lover in person. Later Hardy suggested that their love letters were the equal of those of Robert and Elizabeth Barrett Browning.

When Macmillan rejected *Desperate Remedies* – 'don't touch this', Morley warned, but 'let us see his next story'[135] – Hardy sent it to a lowlier firm, Tinsley Brothers, bypassing Chapman and Hall presumably because he was afraid of learning what Meredith *would have thought of the result of his teaching*.[136] They accepted it immediately, asking only for minor alterations and requesting an advance payment of £75. The revisions were quickly done and the fee (more than half his savings) grudgingly paid out. The novel appeared in March 1871.

Hardy's first wife Emma as a young woman.

*Desperate Remedies* exploits many of the devices of Gothic romance, the sensation novel and detective fiction. Its convoluted plot recounts the romantic adventures of Cytherea Graye through a succession of dangerous and scandalous mysteries and impediments to love, including bigamy, illegitimacy, murder and false identity. Hardy himself disavowed its importance, but it reveals the important link between his frank treatment of social and sexual complications and the forms of popular melodrama.

What little attention it received in the press was, overall, mildly favourable, but in April a notice in the *Spectator* devastated Hardy, and summarily consigned the novel to the remainder list: 'This is an absolutely anonymous story; no falling back on previous works which might give a clue to the authorship, and no assumption of a *nom de plume* which might, at some future time, disgrace the family name ... . By all means let him bury the secret in the profoundest depths of his own heart, out of reach, if possible, of his own consciousness'.[137]

Disheartened as he was, Hardy clung to a couple of reviews that had praised the novel's rustic sketches, and he turned back to his abandoned story of rural life, *Under the Greenwood Tree*. This short idyll is a corrective to *Desperate Remedies* in that it has almost no plot. Instead, it weaves together two stories, one a retelling of the old family story about the demise of the parish church choir, and the other following the ups and downs of a pair of young lovers, Dick Dewy and Fancy Day. At first entitled *The Mellstock Quire*, Hardy laid the emphasis on the quaint and comical doings and sayings of the parish musicians, but when advised by Macmillan's reader (John Morley, later a distinguished politician and biographer) that it lacked dramatic interest he refocused the story around the plot of rival suits for Fancy's hand, re-routing social conflict into sexual conflict, and better attracting, he hoped, readers of commercial fiction.

He had miscalculated, however. *Under the Greenwood Tree* was too short for a three-volume novel, and its submission was badly timed in the lead-up to Christmas. To Hardy's exasperation and disappointment Macmillan liked it, but wouldn't publish it. His only safe recourse was to Tinsley's, and he tentatively informed the firm's principal, William Tinsley, that he had *nearly finished* a *little rural story* but had set it aside at the request of *critic-friends who were taken with D.R.* to make a start on another (much more Tinsleyan, he supposed) novel, *A Pair of Blue Eyes, the essence of which is plot, without crime – but on the plan of D.R.*[138] Unluckily, Tinsley was interested in neither project, only suggesting that when Hardy had another three-volume novel ready, he would publish it, without the £75 guarantee.

Still trapped in his no-man's-land *between literature and architecture*, Hardy despaired of going on, despite Emma's tender encouragement from faraway Cornwall. And truly, the critical moment was approaching. When he finished up with Crickmay he returned to London to work as an architect and was on the verge of giving up fiction when Tinsley finally sent him a cheque for *Desperate Remedies* – as it turned out he lost only £15 on the venture – and asked him to call at his office. There he informed his astonished author that he intended to publish *Under the Greenwood Tree*, and this time he would demand no up-front payment. In fact, *he* would pay Hardy 'the sum of thirty pounds ... one month after publication'.[139] What Hardy didn't realize was that in signing the contract he was signing away his copyright in the novel. It was a decision he later regretted for many reasons, and a mistake he never made again.

*Under the Greenwood Tree* appeared, but Hardy heard nothing more about *A Pair of Blue Eyes* for months until, out of the blue, Tinsley requested a serial novel for his house magazine. Put on the spot, Hardy confessed he had *nothing ready*: *On looking over the MS.,* he wrote back hurriedly, *I find it must have a great deal of reconsideration.*[140] Yet by 15 August, barely a month later, the first instalment of the novel had appeared; by the following March the serial version was finished; and by May 1873 it had been published, with substantial revisions, in three volumes, and bearing, for the first time, his name on the title page.

*A Pair of Blue Eyes* was Hardy's first opportunity to write a novel intended for publication initially as a serial in a popular magazine before being released in volume form. It was a very significant step forward for him: with two sources of income from the one piece of writing, he could afford to give up architecture and live off writing. But it was a gruelling regime, and set the pattern for the next two decades or more of his writing life. He settled to work in St Juliot, the Endelstow of *A Pair of Blue Eyes*, where he had now been courting Emma for 18 months or more. Once again he made one of the protagonists, Stephen Smith, an assistant architect like himself whose father was a rural master-mason and whose mother came from a (supposedly once wealthy and noble) labouring-class family. Like Hardy, Stephen is sent to Cornwall to repair a church tower and must stay with the local vicar and his daughter, the fickle Emma-like Elfride Swancourt, with whom he falls in love. When her father discovers that Stephen's humble family lives close by, he forbids her to marry him: a scene written, no doubt, soon after Emma's father had harshly rejected Hardy's formal proposal of marriage in August 1872. The other protagonist is Henry Knight, a London literary man who represented the kind of man Hardy aspired to be: a sort of Horace Moule, who is a mouthpiece for many of the most

Serialization – publication in separate parts (the free-standing monthly serial, or part issue, popularized by Dickens in the 1830s) and publication in magazine instalments (more dominant from the 1860s) – played an important role in shaping Hardy's fiction. Serials had to keep readers reading from one month to the next, and so relied on incident and suspense. Stories in popular magazines were intended to be read aloud in respectable middle-class families, too, so their content was very strictly controlled.

influential ideas that had been circulating during Hardy's time in London in the 1860s, most especially the new theories of biological and geological time. A version of the 'poor man and the lady' theme, the plot of cross-class sexual relationships is by no means straightforward in *A Pair of Blue Eyes*. The complications and contradictions of Elfride's character – she is virtually a prototype of Hardy's great heroines: flighty, fickle, passionate, intelligent, rebellious, victimized – signals one of Hardy's most important concerns: the interdependence of sexual desire and social power.

Tinsley was happy with *A Pair of Blue Eyes* and predicted great things for his new author, knowing that he could not be satisfied with *Tinsley's Magazine* for long. And already Hardy was thinking ahead to a new project when, on 30 November 1872, he unexpectedly received a letter from Leslie Stephen, the distinguished intellectual and editor of the *Cornhill Magazine*. Stephen was not following *A Pair of Blue Eyes* as it was appearing in *Tinsley's*. The book of Hardy's that had impressed him was *Under the Greenwood Tree*, and, learning of Hardy's identity through Horace Moule, he wrote to congratulate the unknown writer on it, and to request a new novel in the same vein for his magazine.

This was Hardy's big break. Although the *Cornhill* no longer attracted the vast middle-class readership of its early years (Thackeray had been its first editor in 1860), it was still one of the most prestigious and popular fiction magazines in the country. It was also one of the most conservative, and Stephen was, on the face of it, an unusual choice as editor. Intellectually and socially, he had impeccable credentials (Eton and Cambridge), but he was a strident agnostic and a controversialist (significantly, he asked Hardy to witness his renunciation of Holy Orders in 1875), and his opinions on most matters would be sure to offend the anodyne tastes of the *Cornhill*'s readers. Yet surprisingly, perhaps because of his very unorthodoxy, Stephen was rigorously committed to maintaining the magazine's standards. In this respect he was something

Leslie Stephen, editor of the *Cornhill Magazine*, who serialised *Far From the Madding Crowd* in 1873–4.

of a pattern mid-Victorian intellectual. He was a rigorous bowdler-
izer, hyper-sensitive to conventional propriety and careful to commission only the most harmless family fiction. Thus it was that
he approached the author of *Under the Greenwood Tree*; he certainly
never would have chosen the author of the more dangerous and

'Tinsleyan' (as Moule condescendingly described it) *Pair of Blue Eyes*.[141]

Hardy set to work on the new novel – it was to be a pastoral tale, he assured Stephen, about *a young woman-farmer, a shepherd, and a sergeant of cavalry*.[142] The plot of *Far from the Madding Crowd* revolves around four main characters. Gabriel Oak, a small farmer who has lost everything in a freak accident, begins working for the newly arrived mistress of a local farm, Bathsheba Everdene, with whom he falls in love. Boldwood, a wealthy neighbouring gentleman farmer is indifferent to women until Bathsheba sends him a valentine as a joke. The rake Sergeant Troy, whose sexual charm lures Bathsheba into marriage, has abandoned a poor local girl, Fanny Robin, who carries his child, and wanders the countryside in a futile search for him.

By September 1873, Hardy had three chapters ready, and was issued with a contract on the strength of them. In the following months he discovered that Stephen could be difficult, and that there was a price to pay for the privilege of writing for the first rank of mainstream magazines. Stephen was an astute editor, and Hardy benefited from his experience and judgment (he later credited him as *the man whose philosophy was to influence his own for many years, indeed, more than that of any other contemporary*[143]). Where the emerging narrative strayed or threatened to stray onto the dangerous ground of sexual frankness, however, Stephen was unbending. Any suggestion that Fanny Robin was a 'ruined woman' was to be omitted; as was the scene in which Bathsheba finds the baby in Fanny's coffin. Hardy was not in any position to argue, and resigned himself philosophically to his situation. *The truth is*, he wrote to Stephen, *I am willing, and indeed anxious, to give up any points which may be desirable in a story when read as a whole, for the sake of others which shall please those who read it in numbers. Perhaps I may have higher aims some day, and be a great stickler for the proper artistic balance of the completed work, but for the present circumstances lead me to wish merely to be considered a good hand at a serial*.[144] Hardy was so obliging partly because he knew he could always restore the omitted passages for the volume edition (this became his standard practice, although sometimes for various reasons the offending passages never found their way back in). More importantly, though, like other Victorian novelists – George Eliot and Meredith come to mind – he developed covert ways of representing the sexual lives of his characters. Typically of Hardy's visual imagination, these are often vivid vignettes, at once erotically-charged and innocently descriptive, such as the description of Miss Aldclyffe and Cytherea in bed in *Desperate Remedies*, or the cliff-hanging scene in *A Pair of Blue Eyes*, or, in *Far from the Madding Crowd*, the image of Bathsheba dropping suddenly onto her back on her horse to go under the low branches, or the swordplay scene with Troy.

Hardy was working on the first parts of *Far from the Madding Crowd* in Bockhampton during September 1873 when he heard *of the tragic death of his friend Horace Moule, from whom he had parted cheerfully at Cambridge in June*.[145] The depressive, alcoholic Moule had given way to despair, cutting his own throat in his Queen's College bedroom one evening while his brother, who was visiting, read in an adjoining room. This death affected Hardy profoundly. But unlike Tennyson before him (who had the means to devote years to the sacred memory of Arthur Hallam, the subject of *In Memoriam*), Hardy could not afford to be long distracted by his grief for the brilliant, idolized friend of his adolescence and early manhood. Pencil markings in the margins of significant books (including *In Memoriam*), and later poems of Hardy's hint privately at his sorrow and distress. In one poem ('Before My Friend Arrived'), the poet sits by a weir looking across a Frome meadow towards Fordington churchyard and sketching the mound of chalk beside Moule's waiting grave. In another ('Standing by the Mantelpiece'), an erotic subtext is insinuated, entirely in keeping with the passion of Hardy's youthful idolatry, Moule's sexual ambivalence, and the conventions of the elegy.

Julie Christie and Terence Stamp in the 1967 film of *Far from the Madding Crowd*.

If the intensity of his grief carried Hardy back to those days of early promise – a grief experienced among the largely unchanged scenes of his childhood and youth – it inevitably mingled with other memories and feelings of joy and loss that were quickening his imagination as he worked on his new novel in that late summer. It is surely indicative of the happiness and optimism he felt – to have made it as a novelist at last! – that his grief cast no very dark shadows over the comedy of *Far from the Madding Crowd*. He walked to Woodbury-Hill Fair, and depicted it as Greenhill Fair. He chatted with the local old-timers, and wrote, indoors and out, making notes on *large dead leaves, white chips left by the wood-cutters, or pieces of stone or slate that came to hand* – as if the professional writing life really could be at one with the pastoral life.[146] But it was, after all, only for a season: Hardy *assisted at his father's cider-making* for the last time that year, savouring the *sweet smells and oozings in the crisp autumn air*.[147]

Hardy came to associate the writing of *Far from the Madding Crowd* with his own estrangement from the life-ways of his family and community. The new novel depicted a culture in the recent past trying to adjust to almost imperceptible social and economic change in an apparently untouched 'natural' setting, a setting depicted with a poetic fidelity that is both clear-sighted about, and regretful for, its passing. Traditional order is uneasily restored in the novel, in Bathsheba's eventual recognition of Oak's value; but much is left up in the air, particularly surrounding the pregnancy and death of Fanny Robin. By contrast, the beauty of the land itself, shaped by an uninterrupted history of agricultural work – work that generates a whole community of associated trades and skills, social hierarchies and patterns of life – asserts itself magnetically in Hardy's prose, drawing in nostalgic readers alienated by their lives and labours in the towns and cities. This is the pastoral romance that seems to overpower the novel's muted social criticism. We do not see the real social conditions of agricultural labourers in the most deprived county in England at the very time when the trade unionist Joseph Arch was awakening them to political consciousness, as we might in a novel by Gaskell, Dickens or Zola. Yet *Far from the Madding Crowd* is not evasive about social problems. Hardy was looking for a way to explore them that would not commit him to the treatise-like social-problem novel or naturalism.

His approach was understandable, for it reflects his own uneasy place in the modern world, the same sense of homelessness that was to drive him and Emma restlessly from house to house, country to town, for the next decade. An educated urban professional, the country rituals were now only accessible to him as pictures of rustic simplicity and spontaneity from a lost golden age. He was a tourist among his own family. When he needed space and quiet to write, he took the railway home, just as tourists jumped on the train to escape the madding crowd for a week or two. Displacement becomes the dominant theme, plot and device for social critique in Hardy's fiction from *The Poor Man* to *Jude the Obscure*, for his own social displacement was the foundation of his genius as a writer. He understood acutely the predicaments of the *metamorphic classes*,[148] as he called them: those members of anachronistic or in-between rural social formations being overtaken by urban industrial work practices and social structures. Oak, a farmer reduced by ill-fortune to working his way up the social ladder again, exemplifies what for Hardy was a significant and obscured social crisis in the countryside: the dispossession of the relatively poor land-holding classes (the cottagers or liviers: those tradesmen and small farmers whose security depended on renewable lifetime holdings) by changes in work practices brought about by the expansion and rationalization of agricultural production for the fast-growing cities – and especially the need for mobile labour-power. The cottagers represent for Hardy the profound importance of the human investment in place, and his fiction plots the end of permanence and its ways of being. Bathsheba, the landowning daughter of a bankrupt country tailor, points to the centrality of women in the experience of modern displacement. The profound division in Hardy between two incompatible ways of life expresses itself in a sexual restlessness. The overlapping love triangles (Oak–Bathsheba–Troy, Troy–Bathsheba–Boldwood) place the woman between two kinds of men: one naïve and faithful, the other worldly and knowing, contrasting a form of longing for the stability and rightness of the sturdy local culture and its denizens with an unavoidably analytical perspective.

*Far from the Madding Crowd* was a great success with its metropolitan readers. The first instalment appeared in the *Cornhill* on New Year's Eve 1873, and immediately drew high praise in the reviews. The *Spectator*, so contemptuous of *Desperate Remedies*, even conjectured that it was the work of George Eliot – probably 'because you know the names of the stars', Stephen remarked dryly.[149] The novel's success meant that Hardy could at last afford to marry, but it is doubtful whether, after nearly four years' engagement, he was much looking forward to it any more. The families on both sides remained intractably hostile to the union, and the early romance of a love conducted against the wishes of the world faded with time. Writing is a solitary occupation, and the couple's happy early experiences of working together were defeated by the pressures of deadlines and distance. Emma did not even learn about *Far from the Madding Crowd* until the first instalment was published. 'My work', she wrote in July 1874, 'unlike your work of writing, does not occupy my true mind much', adding a little reproachfully: 'Your novel seems sometimes like a child all your own & none of me.'[150] Perhaps, too, he felt something of his heroines' wariness of the finality of marriage – *Love lives on propinquity, but dies of contact*, he noted down in 1889[151] – and was content to prolong the courtship indefinitely. He flirted with other women (Leslie Stephen introduced him to the ebullient Annie Thackeray at about this time), and fell in love again – or, if not, fantasized about it. His illustrator for *Far from the Madding Crowd*, Helen Paterson, was 25 years old, and attractive. Hardy approached her tentatively in 1873, but to no avail. She immediately married another, older man, becoming, to Hardy, another Tryphena Sparks, another lost prize: the woman he ought to have married *but for a stupid blunder of God Almighty.*[152]

In the summer of 1874 he returned to London to await Emma's arrival, and on 17 September they were married at last at St Peter's, Paddington. Emma's uncle the Canon presided, and no one from Hardy's family attended. It was 'a perfect September day', the bride later recalled, 'not brilliant sunshine, but wearing a soft, sunny luminousness'.[153] The newlyweds left immediately for Brighton, *en route* to Rouen in Normandy and Paris, *for materials for my next story,* Hardy informed his brother prosaically – as if, indeed, the journey were all his own and none of Emma. On this and subsequent trips to the Continent, the Hardys were consummate Victorian tourists. Armed with their *Murray's* handbook they were tireless in their sightseeing. Emma, whose gaudy dresses and flamboyant long hair constantly drew the stares of the French, adored Paris, and kept an entertaining travel diary in which she noted the food and clothing, and the peculiarities of the French. On their return, the pair set up house in Surbiton, temporarily, as Hardy thought, but in fact staying until March 1875, when they moved back to his old haunt of the 1860s, the Westbourne Park area near Paddington.

George Eliot (1819–80) rose to fame as a novelist in 1859 with the publication of the pastoral novel *Adam Bede*, set in the fictional Midlands farming county of Loamshire. Her greatest novel, *Middlemarch*, appeared two years earlier than *Far from the Madding Crowd*. Hardy resented the comparison and could not understand it, pointing out that Eliot *never touched the life of the fields: her country-people having seemed to him ... more like small townsfolk than rustics.*[154]

It was important for Hardy to build on his achievement, and Stephen was anxious to capitalize on the popularity of *Far from the Madding Crowd*: he immediately requested a follow-up serial novel. *Desperate Remedies* had been *the unfortunate consequence of Meredith's advice to 'write a story with a plot'.*[155] Now Hardy took *the unfortu-nate course of hurrying forward a further production before he was aware of what there had been of value in his previous one.*[156] Just married, he *had to consider popularity*, but he did not want to be known as a rural regionalist; and *he did not mean to imitate anybody*.[157] R D Blackmore's enormously successful historical romance, *Lorna Doone* (1869), also set in the West Country, had done much to revive the popular regionalism beloved by generations of readers of Sir Walter Scott and Hardy's newfound fans were *apparently expecting him* to go on *writing for ever about sheepfarming*.[158] He was also irritated by the implication that *Far from the Madding Crowd* was in some way derivative of George Eliot; that its very success was testimony to his limitations as a novelist of rural working lives. In response, he embarked defiantly on a metropolitan social comedy, *The Hand of Ethelberta: A Comedy in Chapters*, abandon-ing an idea he had for another country story (later to become *The Woodlanders*).

*Ethelberta* was reasonably well received by its first critics, but was unpopular with readers (and has remained so). Once again Hardy drew on material close to hand – the honeymoon trip to France, various London scenes – but, although Annie Thackeray had reminded him that 'a novelist must necessarily like society', he admitted that he *took no interest in manners, but in the substance of life only*, and was ill-suited to a brittle satire of *modern customs and observances*.[159] Why write the least likely novel then? He was keen to impress Stephen with his versatility and command of styles, and demonstrate his metropolitan sophistication by alluding to the artificial comedy of the 18th century (one of Stephen's specializations).

This is nevertheless a very important novel of Hardy's early period. A failure only insofar as it is so hurriedly and poorly done, and strains to be clever only to seem ham-fisted, it shows an intrepid determination to experiment with form within the strict confines of the middle-class magazine serial and the Mudie's triple-decker. Hardy recognized that these governing conditions were conducive to a bland, unadventurous social fiction, prudish and predictable. His resolution to Stephen, therefore – to eschew *the proper artistic balance* and be *merely ... a good hand at a serial* – hints that, while he was a reliable journeyman who obediently made changes and provided copy on time, he was also interested in pursuing artistic *imbalance*: the lack of proportion, harmony, finish and *taste* that was, to him, essential to a *living style* made out of the struggle between art and actuality.[160] He was anxious to avoid the deadness of fluency. Henry James had derided *Far from the Madding Crowd* for its 'verbose and redundant style', and because it had 'little sense of proportion and almost none of composition': 'Everything human in the book', James wrote, 'strikes us as factitious and insubstantial; the only things we believe in are the sheep and the dogs.'[161] James's genius lay in the novel of manners, and he couldn't possibly recognize that Hardy's genius lay precisely in those markers of social displacement which were, to James, the blemishes of a bad writer. For him, Hardy's inelegance and absence of 'style' were merely vulgar. To Hardy, James's fiction, concerned with *the minutiae of manners*, could only be interesting *when there is nothing larger to think of*.[162] But Hardy knew what he was doing. He confessed to admiring Byron – *a clumsy fellow*, he thought – less for *what he says, than ... what he struggles to say, yet cannot*.[163] In his own case, he sited the expressive power of those clumsy struggles in his *provincialism*. He disagreed with Matthew Arnold, who had decried the provincialism of the English intellect – its eccentric over-enthusiasms untempered by any central cultural authority. For Hardy, a *certain provincialism of feeling is invaluable. It is of the essence of individuality, and is largely made up of that crude enthusiasm without which no great thoughts are thought, no great deeds done.*[164] This is his great originality: to transmute the experience of social displacement and inferiority into an art that was unafraid to risk ineptitude and was never at ease or self-satisfied, unlike, he thought, the *literary productions of men of rigidly good family and rigidly correct education,* [which] *mostly treat social conventions and contrivances – the artificial forms of living – as if they were cardinal facts of life.*[165] 'He is incorrect', Lytton Strachey later wrote; 'but then, how unreal and artificial a thing is correctness! He fumbles; but it is that very fumbling that brings him so near to ourselves.'[166]

Charles Edward Mudie's 'Select Library' in New Oxford St, London, effectively controlled book publishing in Britain between the 1850s and 1890s, and was enormously influential in shaping Victorian fiction. First editions were published in long, expensive three-volume editions intended for purchase by Mudie's to loan to its subscribers. Mudie's was so influential because it filtered out books deemed unsuitable for family reading in the lucrative market of the newly respectable middle classes.

Stephen warned Hardy not to become 'self-conscious and cramped' or lose what was 'perfectly fresh and original about his writing: the 'poetry ... diffused through the prose'.[167] The problem, as Hardy realized, was the popular success of *Far from the Madding Crowd,* which he could not then reconcile with his literary ambition. He was unsure how to combine his native poetic imagination, his hyper-sensitivity to social change and all its ensuing tragic complications and contradictions, and the kind of story a magazine buyer wanted to read. Through the late 1870s and early 1880s, he searched restlessly for the middle ground between commercialism and art, producing poetic and philosophical romances of different moods and forms, and each time failing to reach the popular heights of *Far from the Madding Crowd.* But he remained determined not to build *a reputation for a speciality*, whatever its value to him in income.[168]

In the middle of 1875, the Hardys began searching for houses around Dorset, but not around Dorchester where the influence of Jemima would be overbearing. Eventually they moved to lodgings in Bournemouth, where, oppressed by the endless summer rain, they had a terrible row. As it is recorded in the poem 'We Sat at the Window', it seemed more than just a quarrel, but the beginning of the end: *Wasted were two souls in their prime / And great was the waste, that July time / When the rain came down.*[169] Mortified, they buried their shame and horror and drifted further west to Swanage, on the Purbeck coast, while they hunted for somewhere more permanent and Hardy finished *The Hand of Ethelberta*. In early 1876, when the novel was done, they shifted again to Yeovil, then left for Europe – it was a hot spring on the Continent and Emma found the going hard – only to return home disconsolately to the prospect, as she put it, of 'no home & no chosen county'.[170] After yet more house-hunting, they finally moved to a newly-built villa with a glorious outlook over the Stour River in Sturminster Newton, where they were able to forget the ominous signs of past months. They spent two happy summers at 'Riverside Villa', but the time passed quickly and, characteristically, without Hardy being aware of its enormous significance. In a much later poem, he reflects how unremarkable, even dull, it all seemed – *Yet, all the while, it upbore us like wings / Even in hours overcast: / Aye, though this best thing of things, / 'Nought' it was called!* It was, as it turned out, a sadly truncated beginning: *A preface without any book.*[171] Did Hardy feel this way about Sturminster because it was where the couple had hoped to start a family? Significantly, the most prominent incident remembered from the period in Hardy's biography concerns the pregnancy of their recently dismissed, unmarried servant-girl, whose lover had been secretly visiting in the night: *We hear that Jane, our late servant, is soon to have a baby. Yet never a sign of one is there for us.*[172] The Hardys were past their middle thirties, and would never have children.

It was here that Hardy wrote most of *The Return of the Native*, and began the first of his extensive 'Literary Notebooks', where he recorded ideas and passages of interest and significance to him from his reading of books and the latest periodicals. The notebooks attest to his newfound financial security (from the proceeds of *Ethelberta*), his growing confidence and ambition as a creative artist, and his determination to participate in London intellectual society and keep up his profession, as it were, away from the city. The *Sturminster Newton idyll*[173] also demonstrated once again that Hardy's best writing came out of his close knowledge of the places of his childhood. In *The Return of the Native* he chose to symbolize – indeed personify – the timelessness of Dorset not in the seasonal cycle of pastoral life and work (as in *Far from the Madding Crowd*) but in the imposing physical landscape of Egdon Heath. In reality, Egdon abuts Bockhampton, but in its weirdness and grandeur Hardy's Egdon is a kind of island far from the domesticated farms and hamlets of his family neighbourhood. The setting also freed him to populate the ancient land with a variety of strikingly modern types and their very modern troubles. When Clym Yeobright, the native of the title, returns to Egdon Heath from Paris, his sophistication and exoticism attract the beautiful, fiery Eustacia Vye; she promptly ends her clandestine affair with Damon Wildeve, who hastily and belatedly fulfils his obligation to marry Clym's sister, Thomasin. Clym, however, has come home full of idealism, and eschews personal ambition, much to Eustacia's disgust. They marry, but things do not go well, and the novel is resolved through a series of disastrous mischances. Hardy used what he called the quadrille structure (the rotating inter-involvements of two men and two women) in other plots, too – most famously in *Jude the Obscure*.

In Hardy's original conception of the novel, the characters were not especially marked by social class; but in a series of early revisions he went out of his way to emphasize Mrs Yeobright's gentility, had Clym return from exotic Paris not nearby Budmouth, elevated Wildeve from a local herbalist into that very type of the urban professional, the engineer, and converted Eustacia from a witch's daughter to a naval officer's granddaughter. The rustic

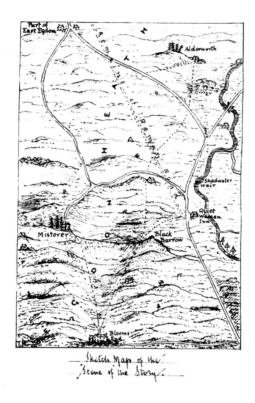

*The Return of the Native*

Sketch Map of the Scene of the Story.

Hardy's sketch map of Egdon Heath for *The Return of the Native*.

chorus is retained in the background, but of all the major characters only Diggory Venn the reddleman, a more mysterious and faintly sinister version of Gabriel Oak who circles around the fringes of the novel, is imbued with old rural values – literally so, the colours of his antique trade (his skin is dyed red from the ochreous pigments he uses to mark sheep) making him stand out as an anthropological curiosity.

Leslie Stephen was wary of the sensationalism of the story – the modernity of its volatile moral restlessness – and Hardy, as if to confirm his editor's prejudices, settled on the much less prestigious *Belgravia*, edited by the sensation novelist Mary Elizabeth Braddon (author of the bestselling *Lady Audley's Secret* and many other novels) for the modest return of £20 per instalment. Nevertheless, this was Hardy's most impressive novel to date, and his chosen venue confirms how close even this ambitious work was to popular melodrama. In it he began to explore artistically many of the issues, ideas, and debates that had so transformed his world in the 1860s, and would continue to occupy his mind for the rest of his life. They are marked by a mood of profound pessimism. For the agnostic Hardy, the decline of religious faith left a gaping hole: an indifferent or malevolent cosmic order, the exact nature of which continued to preoccupy him. He became an acute historian of the *chronic melancholy which is taking hold of the civilized races with the decline of belief in a beneficent Power*.[174] The various rationalist systems and programmes of post-religious thought – utilitarianism and positivism – failed to console him; as did the theories of evolution that promised or presumed the advancement of the human race.

The barren, sparsely inhabited setting of *The Return of the Native*, no place for a comedy of manners, allowed Hardy to abandon pastoral and realism for a distinct hybrid form. On the face of it, humanity has made little or no impression on Egdon. Barely even habitable, livelihoods are sustained there precariously, and social life is severely limited to the few isolated dwellings connected tenuously by almost invisible pathways. Yet the obscure, fleeting domestic dramas of the novel throw massive shadows across this scene of a titanic unconscious nature locked in the aeons of geological time, producing something as grotesque and powerful as Greek tragedy. The heath is a conspicuously theatrical space, lending an Aristotelian unity of place (and time) to a locale which, remote from everyday things, is a natural home to extreme states of being, strong emotionalism, extravagant and improbable actions, and dark plotting. *The Return of the Native* is Hardy's first attempt at a *revived presentation* of *high tragedy*: an *original treatment* in which Nature is unconscious not of *essential laws, but ... those laws framed merely as social expedients by humanity*.[175] Reinterpreted this way, Hardy's tragedy is closer to satire,[176] a mode which allows him to move freely between tragedy and farce, a technique he later perfects in the great novels of the 1880s and 1890s: *If you look beneath the surface of any farce you see a tragedy; and on the contrary, if you blind yourself to the deeper issues of a tragedy you see a farce.*[177]

More even than tragedy or farce, though, *The Return of the Native* may be described as a poetic melodrama, which is the grounding aesthetic of Hardy's greatest fiction. A poet first and foremost, his strongly visual imagination strove after memorable scenic effects: narrative incidents fixed with vivid imagery, succeeding *moments of vision* that demand a story plotted around a succession of crises. In this respect Hardy is a melodramatic writer. Emotions and ideas, contradictions and conflicts are acted out in unexpected or incongruent characters and environments, actions and words. Psychic states and social conflicts are externalized as visual spectacle, using melodramatic conventions borrowed from the sensation novel and the popular stage: hyperbolic gesture, excessive rhetoric, schematic characterization and moral polarization. Women are typically the focus of melodrama, which places its emphasis on the female body and the assumption of men looking at women – a recurrent feature of Hardy's writing. In this regard, Eustacia Vye is the epitome of melodramatic excess. She is a further development of Elfride and Bathsheba, and her body, silhouetted against the night sky, is overburdened with meaning: mythologically overloaded. She is the 'Queen of Night', a pagan goddess who is also a spoiled girl.

There are also strong autobiographical elements in *The Return of the Native*. Hardy described Clym as *the nicest of all my heroes,*

*and* not a bit *like me*[178] – a sure sign of his personal significance –
and created in Mrs Yeobright a mother whose intense, possessive
relationship with her son is clearly reminiscent of Hardy's mother.
Jemima was superstitious and fatalistic in outlook, and suspi-
cious of the world outside Bockhampton. She was openly hostile
towards Emma, and jealously certain that her son would leave his
wife and return home. Her domineering personality and the tight-
knit family she kept close to her were creating serious problems
for the itinerant Hardys in their tentative Dorset interludes. But
Emma was no pushover either, and taking the line that she would
not put up with the social isolation of Sturminster Newton for
much longer, she sent the returned native fleeing back to London
again. The idyll came to an end in March 1878.

There were other motivations for Hardy to leave. He felt,
too, that *the practical side of his vocation of novelist demanded that
he should have his headquarters in or near* London.[179] The desire to
have a presence in the metropolis, to be seen and heard there,
was understandably acute for writers from the countryside: at this
time Hardy ran into Richard Jefferies, the Wiltshire-born author
of *Bevis* (1882) who had, like Hardy, moved up to Surbiton to be
nearer literary London. The Hardys chose a house near Wandsworth Common in Tooting, where they ambitiously took a three-
year lease. He resolved to be accepted by the literary establishment,
and sought election to the Savile Club where he could cultivate
the necessary social, professional and critical connections. He
dined with publishers and editors, attended literary and musical
events, and in 1879 also joined the Rabelais Club, an informal
wining and dining society of literary men founded by the novelist
Walter Besant, and devoted to *virility in literature*.[180] Over the next
months and years he met the great triumvirate of mid-Victorian
poetry – Browning, who had been a major influence on his early
poetic development in the 1860s, Tennyson and Matthew Arnold;
crossed paths with the unsympathetic Henry James; and became

Edmund Gosse (1849–1928), Hardy's most enduring London friend from the 1870s.

friends with the painter Lawrence Alma-Tadema, the actor Henry Irving, and many others.

The most enduring of all his new London friends from the late 1870s was Edmund Gosse, the poet, critic and biographer who

is best remembered now as the author of *Father and Son* (1907),
a harrowing autobiographical account of his upbringing in the
Plymouth Brethren and his troubled relationship with his father.
Gosse was at the centre of virtually every London literary circle
('He would be remembered mainly, he knew, for the people he had
known'[181]). The two men met regularly at the Savile Club, and
in the early years of their friendship Gosse gave safe cover to the
painfully shy Hardy, who 'at first felt overcome by [the] wit and
knowledge' of literary society.[182] He was 'content to bask in Gosse's
beams' during those years, a mutual acquaintance recalled, 'and I
never heard him say anything that couldn't have been said by the
most self-effacing parasite'.[183] Gosse became the most intimate of
all Hardy's correspondents, and one of his great advocates during
the storms of the 1890s (although he was not always publicly
uncritical of Hardy's writing, especially concerning *Jude*).

Hardy spent a good deal of his time in London in the Reading
Room of the British Museum researching the Napoleonic period.
For years he had nursed a grand design for an epic poem on the
war with Napoleon, an *Iliad of Europe from 1789 to 1815*.[184] He
visited ageing war veterans at the Chelsea Hospital and on the
1876 trip abroad saw the Waterloo battlefield for himself. The
epic poem would have to wait, however; for now, he had to make
a living as a writer, and he used his Napoleonic researches in *The
Trumpet-Major*, his only attempt at a genuine historical romance
in the tradition of Scott (most of Hardy's fiction is historical, of
course, in the sense that it is set in an imprecisely dated recent
past). The action of *The Trumpet-Major* takes place in 1804–8. The
Battle of Trafalgar is its distant historical focus, but the novel is
set far from the battlefields in a slightly quaint, antique Georgian
Wessex, where invasion was expected any day. Once again, the
novel is 'the story of one woman in her relations to two or three
men'[185] and once again Hardy approached the *Cornhill* and its
major rivals *Blackwood's* and *Macmillan's Magazine* without success.

The Hardy's house in Trinity Road, Wandsworth Common.

This time, rather pointedly, he chose to place the serial with *Good Words*, an ultra-conservative evangelical magazine – whether as a mild protest to Stephen or not it is impossible to say. That rather odd choice may account for the blandness of *The Trumpet-Major*, published in volume form by Smith, Elder in 1880.

Living and working in London also brought Hardy back into contact with the metropolitan theatre world. He renewed his interest in contemporary interpretations of Shakespeare, regularly seeing Irving, Ada Rehan and Ellen Terry in leading roles over the next two decades. And he continued to be attracted to the popular stage, in particular the music-hall. He would also see a number of Henrik Ibsen's plays when they arrived in England (Gosse was the first English translator and champion of the controversial

Norwegian playwright), finding in Ibsen an exemplar of the artist as oppositional figure and social critic – a vitally important model for the increasing outspokenness of his own fiction in the 1890s. Over the years, Hardy became more and more disaffected with contemporary English drama, however, which privileged, as he saw it, elaborately realistic staging over artistic content.[186] He publicly scorned writing for the stage; but he was in fact, like many of his contemporaries, drawn to its glamour, wide popular reach, and money. He developed many outlines and scenarios for plays adapted from his own fiction, but few of them came to anything. His earliest experience of working in the theatre in the 1860s had been unpromising, and his first effort at dramatization, in the late 1870s and early 1880s, can hardly have encouraged him further. In collaboration with a playwright, J Comyns Carr, he turned *Far from the Madding Crowd* into *Mistress of the Farm* for the St James's Theatre, who rejected it, privately commissioning Arthur Wing Pinero, one of the leading commercial playwrights of the day, to write a derivative treatment, *The Squire*, instead. A furore resulted, with indignant letters to the *Times*, and counter-accusations of incidents of plagiarism in *The Trumpet-Major*. In response, Carr hurriedly rewrote the play as *Far from the Madding Crowd*. It was not a success. Hardy's fiction is ideally suited to film and television, with their lush, lingering visuals; but it never adapted well to the stage, perhaps because he sought *a balance between the uncommon and the ordinary so as on the one hand to give interest, on the other to give reality. The uncommonness*, he concluded, *must be in the events, not in the characters*.[187] On stage, that uncommonness of event can seem static and unintentionally comical. Stripped of its scenic descriptive prose, the fiction becomes both undramatic (the action is episodic and constantly waylaid by excursions into rusticity) and paradoxically too *melo*dramatic.

In July 1880 the Hardys holidayed in France, and Hardy began preparations for a serial destined for a brand new publishing venture by the American firm of Harper and Brothers, who were planning a London-based European edition of their monthly magazine. He had completed three instalments of *A Laodicean* when he fell suddenly and mysteriously ill with a bladder disease. The specialist who attended him ordered him either to have surgery – an idea which terrified him – or rest in bed until he was well. He stayed there, with his feet higher than his head, from November 1880 until May 1881. Because he had no intention of letting *Harper's* know of his illness, he doggedly and painfully dictated the remainder of *A Laodicean* to Emma.

In June 1881, just weeks after leaving the house for the first time in six months, the Hardys packed up and left London again. They had spent more than three years in the Tooting house, where *their troubles began* in earnest.[188] London oppressed him and made him ill, just as it had in the 1860s. One morning during those years he had woken early, feeling *that I had not enough staying power to hold my own in the world*.[189] On another occasion, looking down on the busy streets he had imagined the crowd as *a molluscous black creature* that took *the shape of the streets* and threw out *horrid excrescences and limbs into neighbouring alleys*.[190] And looking over the city from the high ground of the Tooting house, he was haunted by *an eerie feeling*, a *horror at lying down in close proximity to 'a monster whose body had four million heads and eight million eyes'*.[191] Worst of all, he discovered that *residence in or near a city tended to force mechanical and ordinary productions from his pen, concerning ordinary society-life and habits*.[192] Surely, he reasoned, this was because *I find that a certain defect in my nature hinders my working abreast with others of the same trade. Architecture was distasteful to me as soon as it became a shoulder to shoulder struggle – literature is likewise – & my only way of keeping up a zest for it is by not mixing with other workers of the same craft*.[193]

Unsurprisingly, *A Laodicean* is the most mechanical and ordinary of Hardy's novels. But like so many of his failed experiments, it is also full of interest. A philosophical romance of architecture, it is subtitled a *story of to-day*, and mixes a sensational and melodramatic plot of intrigue and double-dealing, complete with stagy villains, and a farcical comedy of manners in the 18th-century style of *Ethelberta*, all in the service of a long meditation on medievalism and modernity. The novel begins strikingly with a humming telegraph wire that George Somerset, the lukewarm hero referred to in the title, traces back to its source, a rotting medieval castle now owned by the thoroughly modern heroine, Paula Power ('Miss Steam-Power'). Notwithstanding its undeniable though understandable flaws, *A Laodicean* is a fascinating novel that looks forward to *Tess of the d'Urbervilles* in its exploration of the ambivalence of the past, the decay of family lines and the stress of the modern.

After stopping briefly in Dorchester, the Hardys moved into 'Llanherne', a newish brick villa close to the railway station in Wimborne on the Stour river. It was here that Hardy, now in his early forties, finally settled on a lifestyle that was satisfactory to him as a writer whose creative energies were refocusing onto Dorset and the south-west and who needed to keep closely in touch with London literary culture. At Llanherne the Hardys established themselves as a solidly and comfortably middle-class couple – part of the town establishment – taking pride and pleasure in their garden and conservatory, attending local dinners, balls and Shakespeare readings, taking holidays abroad, touring the local area, and, in the spring and summer of 1883, going up to London on the train: an annual ritual that they would continue for 30 years.

In Wimborne, Hardy wrote the last of the novels that make up the first phase of his writing career, novels that are all, in one way or another, influenced by the same *modern vice of unrest* that had plagued him and Emma throughout the first decade of their marriage as they vacillated between London and Dorset, at home in neither place. Like its predecessor, *Two on a Tower* is a philosophical comedy of manners which modulates, or degenerates, into a sensational romance, and takes astronomy as its dominant trope as *A Laodicean* had taken architecture. Hardy's own projected advertisement for the novel describes its melodramatic plot perfectly: *Being the story of the unforeseen relations into which a lady and a youth many years her junior were drawn by studying the stars together; of her desperate situation through generosity to him; and of the reckless* coup d'audace *by which she effected her deliverance* (the heroine, Viviette, who is pregnant by the young hero, dupes a bishop into marrying her).[194] Parts of it are extraordinary, especially where it takes up again the themes and images of human insignificance from *The Return of the Native*, meditating upon the *ghastliness* of night, when *there is nothing to moderate the blow with which the infinitely great, the stellar universe, strikes down upon the infinitely little, the mind of the beholder*.[195] But as Hardy confessed to Gosse, *though the plan of the story was carefully thought out, the actual writing was lamentably hurried* without him having a chance to see the proofs (it was published in America in the *Atlantic Monthly*). He ought perhaps to have rewritten it, too, for publication in book form, as he admitted sheepishly, but had played truant and gone off on holiday to Paris instead – to say nothing of the regular house-hunting, and Wimborne and London social commitments. The novel caused an uproar, as Hardy seems to have hoped, but it was all quickly forgotten. In the eight years since his marriage in 1874 he had written steadily, completing five novels and a number of short stories. He was a capable skilled tradesman in a small way – a *good hand at a serial* who made a modest living. He had made a name, but so far only as the author of *Far from the Madding Crowd*.

# Novelist 1883–97

In April 1883 Hardy's novels were the subject of a long, discerning survey in the prestigious quarterly *Westminster Review* by Havelock Ellis (later famous as a sexual psychologist, critic and social reformer), who predicted with some regret that Hardy was now unlikely to 'write another novel of the peculiar power, and ... peculiar weakness, of *Far from the Madding Crowd*'.[196] The 'vein of comedy' that ran through *A Laodicean* and *Two on a Tower* was, Ellis wrote, probably the 'most characteristic outcome of his genius'.[197] Despite strong continuities between the earlier and later novels – all Hardy's stories were love-stories involving heroines unmistakably his own, and his distinctive style managed to 'touch the extreme verge of dramatic vividness'[198] – Ellis found each novel 'a new point of departure and a new development'. Hardy seemed gradually to have left behind the 'intimate knowledge of rural life' that he had introduced into the English novel: the 'love and art which bind him to the familiar heath-land of Wessex'.[199]

In fact, when Ellis's article was appearing, Hardy had already decided – and Emma had acquiesced, although neither of them were enthusiastic about the prospect – to find or build a house somewhere in the neighbourhood of that very heath-land. By this time, too, Hardy was taking stock of his career and planning to take his fiction in an entirely unexpected new direction, away from the quirky 'problem' comedies and back to the romance of Dorset rural life. In ten years his work had become increasingly adventurous and increasingly unpopular. Ellis was admiring, but many of Hardy's readers were wearying of his cleverness and advanced views, so his decision to reinvent himself as the custodian of *a fairly true record of a vanishing life* and simultaneously the creator of a people *meant to be typically and essentially those of any and every place where / 'Thought's the slave of life, and life time's fool'*[200] was strongly based on a pragmatic view of his future and a considered reassessment of his strengths as an artist. His reputation and popularity still rested almost exclusively on *Far from the Madding Crowd*; and his one and only attempt at a carefully planned work of art, as distinct from a hastily written and inevitably compromised commercial serial, was *The Return of the Native*. These were both novels of his home countryside; yet they were nothing like each other. There was rich scope for artistic experiment here. If the size of the agricultural workforce had been halved by a century of industrial expansion, nevertheless England remained more rural in the period between 1850 and 1880, when most of Hardy's fiction is set, than we tend to think.[201] The great subject of his later fiction, the effects of modernity in the countryside, was acutely visible to him in his own emblematically modern life. If he felt himself *in a sense exiled*,[202] he could at least write about Dorset without feeling, as he had in the 1870s, that he would be dismissed as a minor regionalist, or that he had lessened himself as an artist.

In late 1882, he was busy mining family history and local history, systematically studying old copies of the *Dorset County Chronicle* and recording unusual or striking incidents in a 'Facts' notebook for possible use in future novels. This new enthusiasm for local historical research, while it shows up Hardy's disconnectedness from his own past, also reminds us that his family and their neighbours also no longer lived in the old remote life-ways of their forebears. As T S Eliot recognized, 'Hardy wrote of the Dorset that was already passing in his boyhood', and had virtually disappeared by about 1865.[203] Jemima's memory was prized not because it maintained the traditions of an oral culture, therefore, but because she was a living historian of a departed way of life. She embodied that absolute break between tradition and modernity that Hardy saw as taking place in Dorset over the course of a single generation.

Dorset was unique in that it was one of the last agricultural counties in the south to feel the effects of industrial modernity. But it was unique, too, in its countryside, at that time largely unappreciated by outsiders. Its sheer geological diversity and variable patterns of land-use offered a variety of landscape regions that differed absolutely from each other. The novelist, like the tourist, could exploit these differences. Each of the five novels Hardy wrote after 1883 took its dominant complexion from an aspect of the Dorset geography: the county town and its hinterland (*The Mayor of Casterbridge*); the woodlands to the north (*The Woodlanders*); Blackmore Vale, the rich heathland valleys of the Frome, and the central chalk uplands (*Tess of the d'Urbervilles*); the heavy claylands of the north (*Jude the Obscure*); and the limestone promontory, Portland Bill (*The Well-Beloved*). Extended to the half-dozen counties which he *reunited under the old name of Wessex* with Dorset its centre-point, what became known as the 'Hardy country' was, as he later pointed out, not much smaller than Ancient Greece. A literature confined to a regional landscape need not after all confine the imagination.

All these factors came together to induce Hardy to take the step he had resisted for so long. He succumbed to the needs of his own imagination by settling in Dorchester and recommencing the fiction of country life in earnest. He could do so because he didn't need to go on proving himself in London as a clever novelist of manners: the metropolitan man of letters who could never quite shake off that 'decided accent of some kind'.[204] He began *The Mayor of Casterbridge* in a rented house in the county town while he waited for his father's firm, now run by his brother Henry, to build him a house on a substantial plot of land purchased from the Duchy of Cornwall about a mile from town on the Wareham Road.[205] The Hardys quickly established themselves in their temporary accommodation in Shire-Hall Place, a rambling house in a lane behind High West Street. They set up just as they had in Wimborne as a comfortable and cultured middle-class couple, receiving local and London visitors despite the small-town gossip of those who, like Arthur Shirley all those years before, still scorned the upstart. Regardless of Hardy's own buried feelings of inferiority, and Emma's later, bitter claim that 'A man who has humble relations shouldn't live in the place where he was brought up',[206] his social status in Dorchester was in fact relatively secure. He was appointed as a local magistrate (later ascending to the county bench) and became more active in the Dorset Natural History and Antiquarian Field Club. When the builders, digging the foundations for the new house, began unearthing Romano-British relics, Hardy took a close interest and presented a paper detailing the finds to the Club. And when the new Dorset County Museum opened in January 1884 under the curatorship of Horace Moule's brother, he made frequent use of its facilities in his researches.

As it turned out, the house, Max Gate, was a miraculous compromise. The remote village and town life of Hardy's parents and siblings would not do for a man whose intellectual, professional and social status was tied to London; but London could not be borne. On the outskirts of Dorchester, Hardy was close to the vital sources of his imagination, but a measured distance from Bockhampton and Jemima's imperious presence. The house was named after a turnpike that once stood on the road outside, which had in turn been named after the original turnpike-keeper (maps still referred to it as 'Mack's Gate' in 1902). It was built on an isolated and exposed spot high above the surrounding country, well away from neighbours and the noise of the busy market-town, where Hardy could work without interruptions or distractions. At the same time – and the following description in an 1888 magazine article was probably written from Hardy's own notes – it was just 'a short walk by foot-path from the railway which will deliver him in London within four hours, so that he is more often in the bustling world than would be inferred from the seclusion of his "writing-box", as he calls this house'.[207]

Hardy found it unnerving at first to own something so permanent as a red-brick villa on an acre and a half. Six months after moving in, he wondered in his diary whether it had been *a wise expenditure of energy*,[208] and ten years later he was still considering whether to stay.[209] But it was convenient and private, and Max Gate remained his home for the rest of his life. As originally planned, the house was designed, with its oddly small-windowed turret, to take advantage of the *extensive view of the surrounding country*.[210] But while it was being built, Hardy planted rows of Austrian pines along the boundary as a windbreak to protect the house and gardens, create privacy, and provide shelter for birds and wildlife in the winter. He also put in beeches and sycamores, hornbeams and elms along the windward side of the circular drive. For nearly two decades, the house remained conspicuous in its grounds. But over time the trees reached maturity. Hardy was always sensitive to the sufferings of living things and could not bear to prune them or cut them down, and they began to enclose the property claustrophobically, throwing the house into darkness in the winters.

Max Gate has few admirers. It is described in Pevsner's *Buildings of England* as a house of 'no architectural qualities whatever'.[211] There is something ungainly and meanly utilitarian, even institutional, about its eclectic plum brick exterior. Its display of solidity and respectability is palpable, and yet it remains as obdurately incongruous in the built-up landscape now, softened by creepers and established gardens, as it had when it was 'raw new'.[212] Hardy's choice of the building materials of the new suburbs in favour of the mellower local stone is symptomatic of his refusal to be identified with the *merely* local. Rather, as he put it later in his biography, the house was built as the *country quarters* of a professional London man.[213] At the same time, if its outside bluntly declared the permanence of the returned native's raised social standing, inside it was unaffected and simple, designed for plain living and high thinking. There was a flushing toilet, but no bathroom until 1920. Hardy made two major additions to the structure, extending the kitchen, adding bedrooms and twice relocating his study. It was a house designed for the daily routine of writing, which Hardy religiously observed. It was also a house sadly missing the vibrancy and disorderliness of family life. It 'seems so quiet,' Nellie Gosse wrote to her daughter Tessa from Max Gate, 'with no little ones running about and shouting'.[214]

The Hardys' decision to settle in Dorchester coincided with a momentous change in their social lives. In the summer of 1884 Hardy was taken up by the influential matrons of the wealthy landed classes and invited to London for the Season in June and July. Lady Portsmouth; the Duchess of Abercorn; the Countess of Carnarvon; Lady Hilda Broderick; the Marchioness of Londonderry; and most especially Mary Jeune, who was a journalist and charity worker as well as a society hostess, and became a close friend of Hardy's: these women led the new cosmopolitanism in social London in the 1880s. Then, fashionable society opened its doors to a new element – members of the professions, painters, actors, literary and scientific men and women. It is important to recognize that Hardy was not a lone recruit to this rarefied company. The writers and artists he saw, met and mixed with there were all themselves relative newcomers in the previously exclusive titled circles in the 1880s: Walter Pater, Matthew Arnold, Henry James, Gosse and his friend the sculptor Hamo Thornycroft, and Thornycroft's brother-in-law, Lawrence Alma-Tadema, the painter – even Oscar Wilde. It was an age of political and imperial crisis, of domestic unrest and Irish nationalist hostility. But as Mary Jeune remembered it, 'society in London in the eighties was very agreeable ... because it had become more cosmopolitan, and people generally took a greater interest in political questions, while there was a sharp division between political parties. Nothing divided society like the Home Rule Question, so that if one's acquaintances comprised people on both sides, it gained much in interest and amusement'.[215] There was a feeling of momentous change in the air, an energy that Hardy was keen to observe closely. He was still planning his Napoleonic epic, with its interplay of great historical players and nonentities, and he spent much of his summers watching influential men at the *nominally social but really political parties*,[216] and in the long disputatious sittings of the House of Commons. He searched the performances of Gladstone and Joseph Chamberlain for clues to the characters of public men under enormous pressure, as Pitt and Fox had been in the face of Napoleon's advances. As he did so, he came to the conviction that history was not made by great minds or momentous decisions, but was *in the main the outcome of* passivity – *acted upon by unconscious propensity*.[217] *The offhand decision of some commonplace mind high in office at a critical moment influences the course of events for a hundred years*,[218] he noted, beginning to think of these historical actors as sleepwalkers, and society as a gathering of *beings in a somnambulistic state, making their motions automatically – not realizing what they mean*.[219]

A poor man among the ladies and a provincial free-trade Liberal among the Tories, Hardy might well have thought of himself as sleepwalking through all the 'crushes' and 'small-and-earlies' of the summer Seasons. The novelist George Gissing, visiting Max Gate in 1895, was irritated by Hardy's constant talk of 'fashionable society' and 'lords & dignitaries'.[220] In the *Life*, moreover, written nearly 30 years later, Hardy hides himself during his most important creative period – a time of growing frustration, alienation, anger and despondency – behind a flurry of name-dropping and gazetting of social calls and parties. In the eyes of the powerful men he met, he was doubtless as politically inconsequential as the women with whom he almost exclusively associated, but he was strongly attracted to power, and relished these opportunities for professional advancement and social elevation. But he could not remain unaffected by the deep contradictions between these glittering interludes and the life he lived at home, with its very different views of the world. The situation led inevitably to an uneasy rationalization of his political convictions and a cynicism about politics. *Conservatism is not estimable in itself*, he remarked, as if to argue away the problem, *nor is Change, or Radicalism. To conserve the existing good, to supplant the existing bad by good, is to act on a true political principle, which is neither Conservative nor Radical.*[221] The bureaucratic bungling that led to the death of General Gordon and the fall of Khartoum in 1885, and the political machinery that drove the Irish Home Rule debates, seem to have been turning-points for him.[222] In the end he described himself as *neither Tory nor Radical* but *an Intrinsicalist*: someone *against privilege derived from accident of any kind* and therefore *equally opposed to aristocratic ... and democratic privilege.*[223]

Hardy especially disapproved of the arrogance of working-class majority rule. He believed that *Opportunity should be equal for all, but those who will not avail themselves of it should be cared for merely – not be a burden to, nor the rulers over, those who do avail themselves thereof.*[224] Like other late-Victorian intellectuals (most notably his friend Edmund Gosse, who feared that 'poetry is dead, the novel sunken into its dotage, all good writing obsolete, and the reign of darkness begun'[225]), he feared for the future of art in a majority-rule working-class democracy. In April 1891, he visited the British Museum and found *Crowds parading and gaily traipsing round the mummies, thinking to-day is for ever, and the girls casting sly glances at young men across the swathed dust of Mycerinus {?}. They pass with flippant comments the illuminated MSS. – the labours of years – and stand under Rameses the Great, joking. Democratic government may be justice to man, but it will probably merge in proletarian, and when these people are our masters it will lead to more of this contempt, and possibly be the utter ruin of art and literature!*[226]

Back in 1883 Hardy's return to Dorchester and the fiction of rural life prompted him to write an essay, 'The Dorsetshire Labourer', which dealt with the vanishing ways of life of local rural workers, and aimed to intervene directly in the question of working-class suffrage at a time when the condition of agricultural labourers and the debate over rural electoral reform were highly politicized and controversial topics. It is an important sketch, too, for the rural social world Hardy was about to represent in a succession of novels and stories, and is extremely revealing about his own situation. He perceived that agricultural labourers, even in forfeiting their old title of 'workfolk', had already begun to absorb themselves into the urban working classes: a group defined by a common oppression and common political aims, not by its hierarchical relation to those above it in rural communities whose interests it shared. New work practices, however, had brought about that change: now, the *sojourning existence of the town masses is more and more the existence of the rural masses.*[227] The itinerancy of labourers forced to find work wherever they could at the hiring fairs was never, in Hardy's mind, separate from the systematic evictions of that *better-informed class, ranking distinctly above {the labourers} – the blacksmith, the carpenter, the shoemaker, the small higgler, the shopkeeper ..., together with nondescript workers other than farm-labourers.*[228] This was his family's class, the 'cottagers' who had settled on their life-holds a generation or two earlier. Never comfortably off, they depended upon the landowners as completely as the field-labourers did. There was always the risk of falling into poverty; and, as landowners allowed more life-holds to lapse between 1840 and 1880, more and more cottagers were forced out of their villages. *This process*, Hardy wrote in a passage he later reused in *Tess*, *is designated by statisticians as 'the tendency of the rural population towards the large towns',* but *is really the tendency of water to flow uphill when forced.*[229] In this way Hardy elided the fate of the agricultural labouring class with the tragic fate of his own class, thereby virtually effacing from his Wessex the unionized workers who were uniting against their landed oppressors. Yet it is true that the fate of the cottagers did have a tremendous impact on the culture of countryside: communities stripped of shops and services struggled then, as they do today, to survive. As a direct result, rural people *lost touch with their environment, and that sense of long local participancy which is one of the pleasures of age*: an apt description of Hardy's own itinerant circumstances through the 1870s and 1880s – a restless sojourner.[230]

Hardy's first Dorchester novel begins with the striking image of a morose hay-trusser walking in absolute silence along an empty Dorset highway with his wife and baby. Michael Henchard's precise social identity is established immediately in his clothing, tools, and gait: *His measured, springless walk was the walk of the skilled countryman as distinct from the desultory shamble of the general labourer.* Significantly, the new novel, *The Mayor of Casterbridge*, was not a love story but a study of Henchard: the *man of character* with whose life and death it deals. It appeared in the *Graphic*, a widely circulating weekly pictorial news magazine (similar to the *Illustrated London News*). In May 1886 it was published, considerably revised, in book form by Smith, Elder and Co.

In *The Mayor of Casterbridge* and throughout the succeeding 'novels of character and environment' Hardy reintroduces key story elements from *Far from the Madding Crowd* and *The Return of the Native*. The most notable of these is the intrusive arrival of a figure emblematic of modern life from far beyond the enclosed horizon of the rural community. Psychologically and symbolically, however, these figures – Bathsheba and Troy in *Far from the Madding Crowd*; Wildeve and the returning Clym in *The Return of the Native*; Farfrae and Lucetta in *The Mayor of Casterbridge*; Fitzpiers, Mrs Charmond and the returning Grace Melbury in *The Woodlanders*; Angel Clare and Alec d'Urberville in *Tess* – do not represent modes of being altogether unheard-of among, or unwished for by, the locals. In fact they appear at the interface of two very modern desires: for economic and social advancement by the complex and diverse rural lower classes; and for a much vaunted rural simplicity by educated, leisured urbanites disillusioned with, and often made cynical by, capitalist modernity. *The Mayor of Casterbridge* is set in the middle years of the 19th century, when Hardy was growing up in Dorchester, and the county town is depicted as an insular pre-modern economy and society, which even the railway has not reached. Yet the deeply conservative Henchard, set in his old ways, feels an unexpected kinship with the young stranger, Farfrae, who is passing through Casterbridge on his way to the new world, and detains him (as Angel is later detained by the May dance in Marlott by his erotic fascination for *rustic unsophistication*[231]). The mayor is a physically powerful man, hot-headed, impulsive and instinctual in all his dealings. Farfrae, by contrast, while open and friendly, is cool and detached in matters of business and pleasure, with a rational mind deft in the application of general rules and systems to the specifics of local commerce. His abstract universal knowledge is the very antithesis of Henchard's raw, materially felt local knowledge (the capacity or weakness for abstraction is a characteristic of all Hardy's intrusive moderns). Henchard little realizes that he has willed his own destruction in his determination that Farfrae should stay – it is the inevitable willed self-destruction of the pre-modern by the modern: for who could resist what Hardy in *The Return of the Native* calls *the irrepressible New*?[232] – and the novel traces the old-time mayor's decline into extinction.

At the same time, Farfrae's name captures his real meaning wonderfully well by anticipating the absent word 'home': what he is destined to be 'far frae'. This suggests the easygoing adaptability and rootlessness of the entrepreneur, and the opportunism at the bottom of his commercial success. Farfrae sings passionately about his motherland, but with the kind of sentimental attachment that is only possible because he has no intention of ever returning to its awful primitive conditions. He is the homeless modern *par excellence*, whose arrival signals the beginning of the corrosion of Casterbridge as its own place: as *home* to its inhabitants. Henchard's Casterbridge is unique; Farfrae's Casterbridge is nowhere in particular – any market town where food commodities are traded. As Casterbridge gratefully embraces modern ways, Henchard declines into an atavism, wasting away in his decaying mud cottage on the other side of Egdon Heath.

Hardy had settled on a neat prescription for tragedy shortly after writing *The Return of the Native*, arguing in 1878 that it *should arise from the gradual closing in of a situation that comes of ordinary human passions, prejudices, and ambitions, by reason of the characters taking no trouble to ward off the disastrous events produced by the said passions, prejudices, and ambitions.*[233] While working on *The Mayor of Casterbridge* he made a further observation: that tragedy *exhibits a state of things in the life of an individual which unavoidably causes some natural aim or desire of his to end in a catastrophe when carried out.*[234] But what state of things could lead to such an unavoidable catastrophe? Hardy was, as Irving Howe once argued, an earnest doubter who 'had to make his plots convey the oppressiveness of fatality without positing an agency determining the course of fate'. As a result he often 'seems to be plotting against his own characters'.[235] Certainly all of Hardy's fiction from *The Mayor of Casterbridge* onwards views life as a *drama of pain* in which *happiness was but* an *occasional episode.*[236] And, taken together, these novels constitute *an account of human action in spite of human knowledge, showing how very far conduct lags behind the knowledge that should really guide it.*[237] We can see Hardy slowly approaching that *history of human automatism, or impulsion* that would be most fully and philosophically treated in *The Dynasts*.

Hardy had invested a lot in this tragic novel of Dorchester. Henchard, despite his 'shrewd, proud, illiterate, primitive nature',[238] is Lear-like with his larger-than-life frame, immoderate temper, and massive follies and humiliations. His fate is explicated through a profound Darwinian vision of the survival of the fittest, a vision in keeping with the novel's archaeological layerings of pagan and Biblical discourse and the language of political economy. *The Mayor of Casterbridge* magisterially dwarfs Hardy's immediately previous experiments in comedy and the problem novel of ideas (what he came to call his 'romances and fantasies' and 'novels of ingenuity'). Deliberately seasoned with references to characters and settings from *Far from the Madding Crowd*, it looks back to the past, but offers a striking new approach.

Hardy met George Gissing (1857–1903) in July 1886, when the younger novelist was struggling to find his way, and was making contacts in literary society as Hardy himself had done. Gissing was intent on pursuing *literature as distinct from the profession of letters*,[239] but where for Hardy *the heart of literature* was poetry[240] for Gissing it was the novel. He was a driven man, a perfectionist who was crushed by the commercial market which he depended upon, but which was indifferent to his art. His greatest novel, *New Grub Street* (1891), earned him a mere £150.

After the deaths of George Eliot (1880) and Trollope (1882), Hardy entered the last phase of his career as a novelist with the field wide open before him. Meredith was now the pre-eminent figure, but did not command the wide readership of his predecessors. A new generation was coming through, initiating the 'great divide' between serious literature and popular romance that would culminate in modernism. On the one side, George Gissing, Henry James and George Moore; and on the other, Rider Haggard, Walter Besant, Hall Caine and Marie Corelli – and between them Robert Louis Stevenson and the phenomenon that was Rudyard Kipling, shortly to burst onto the scene: the star of the East, as Gosse dubbed him.[241]

Stevenson had not yet met Hardy, but he wrote enthusiastically asking if he might adapt *The Mayor of Casterbridge* for the stage. Hardy was flattered, but remained uneasy about the novel's reception. He had contrived stopgap plot devices to circumvent the censorship of sexual matters in the *Graphic*, and weekly serialization had overburdened the story with incidents, perhaps permanently damaging it. The process of revision became overwhelming, and Hardy put it off until the last minute. It seemed almost impossible to retrieve the work he had set out to write. *I fear it will not be so good as I meant*, he noted to himself anxiously.[242] And surprisingly, it was on the whole indifferently received. Ironically, because of its steady focus on Henchard's 'homely grandeur'[243] and tragic decline – 'Round him all its interest centres, and with him it ends'[244] – *The Mayor of Casterbridge* is one of Hardy's most unified novels. Ironically, too, throughout the next decade Hardy's growing artistic ambitions for his fiction were decisively shaped by, indeed they owe something of their greatness to, the disabling conditions of serial publication. The structural integrity of his next novel was compromised even more than the *Mayor*; yet *The Woodlanders*, on which he had been working since late 1885, was an outstanding critical success. This was the novel, or at least the story, Hardy had originally intended to follow *Far from the Madding Crowd* a decade earlier but had abandoned for the *Ethelberta* experiment, and it has strong continuities with the earlier novel's loving depiction of a landscape with strong personal associations. *The Woodlanders* is set in the north-west of Dorset, in the densely wooded country around High Stoy Hill and Melbury Osmond where his mother had grown up.

*The Woodlanders* was not an easy novel to write. Without the luxury of *The Mayor*'s long lead time, it had to be produced under the extreme pressure of serial deadlines, and Hardy seems to have been uncertain how to weave together the various narratives, and which should be given precedence. In the early planning stages

Hardy in 1884, with what Ford Madox Ford called his 'elder-statesman's beard'.

he worked for hours every day in *a fit of depression* trying to get the details right, finally settling on the *original plot ... after all*.[245] The focus of his first title, *Fitzpiers at Hintock*, on the adventures of the philandering dilettante implies that Hardy had quite different ideas about, or greater ambitions for, this new story of evolutionary struggle, and rural decline and change. But the difficulty of investing such an unprepossessing anti-hero with the necessary gravity must have shown Hardy the doubtful promise of this direction, although one can imagine what the Europeans – Flaubert, say, or Maupassant – might have done with Fitzpiers and the story of his 'shameless falsehood, levity and infidelity, followed by no true repentance'.[246] After Henchard, however, and with serious constraints on Hardy's time, a follow-up story about a man of little character must have seemed too much to attempt, and there are no other obvious heroes. He wisely chose to make the woodland landscape the hero of the novel.

The action of *The Woodlanders* takes place for the most part behind a dense *screen of boughs*, in the congested green undergrowth where pathways and roads are *made ragged by* [the] *drip and shade* of overhanging branches, and villages are *sequestered* – hidden deeply away in the woods, as if hidden from the present. The landscape around Little Hintock is wet and fertile. It is fine country for timber and apple growing, and richly redolent of traditional cultures and old lore: the refuge of *the fruit-god and the wood-god*.[247] But the old highway that once linked the village to its nearby markets and the wider world is empty except for occasional pedestrians and local carts – it has been superseded by the railway – and Little Hintock, *outside the gates of the world*,[248] is that vanishing place so beloved of the tourist and the anthropologist.

There are obvious echoes of *Far from the Madding Crowd* here, in the homecoming of Grace Melbury, who is yet another returning native changed by her schooling abroad and her father's ambitions for her; the arrival of the decadent outsiders, Fitzpiers – an idle, dissipated refugee from the *beau-monde* – and (shortly afterwards) Félice Charmond, the mysterious cosmopolitan heiress; and the fateful steadfastness of the sturdy, unlucky peasant lovers, Giles Winterborne and Marty South. Once again Hardy explores the encounter between 'a woman lifted by circumstances a little out of [her] sphere – educated too highly for it, rendered too fine for it, yet excluded from a superior status'[249] and the outwardly classless urban professional drop-out who cultivates a phoney leisured traditionalism to free himself for an easy career of sexual predation. Moreover the complex pattern of romantic entanglements – Marty loves Giles, who loves Grace, who marries Fitzpiers, who absconds with Mrs Charmond – repeats and complicates the pattern of earlier novels (in *The Return of the Native*, Diggory Venn loves Thomasin, who loves Wildeve, who loves Eustacia, who loves Clym). Once again, it is the erotic force-field of human relationships that interests Hardy, the motive energy of a dance of automatons, all of them partners in each other's fates as they revolve and cross in their interdependent orbits.

The comedic impulse of *Far from the Madding Crowd* has gone from *The Woodlanders*, however; and nor do the woods, despite their tremendous symbolic presence, offer the sombre, eerily rarefied tragic unity of the heathland landscape in *The Return of the Native*. Early on, the narrator claims that the Hintock woods were conducive to *dramas of a grandeur and unity truly Sophoclean*. But *The Woodlanders* is one of those late tragedies of Hardy's (*Jude* is another) that comes 'dangerously near to farce', just as *The Return of the Native* had.[250] Since *Desperate Remedies* Hardy had been refining a technique that juxtaposed a powerfully involving realism of *setting* – achieved by what a reviewer of that first novel had described as his 'sensitiveness to scenic and atmospheric effects'[251] – with a powerfully disruptive (and, to contemporary readers, compelling) melodrama of *incident*. *The Woodlanders* is 'less vividly sensational' and in a more 'subdued key',[252] and it finely balances social comedy and pathos. Realism is put to a meticulous and loving representation of place, and the intricate local forms of social organization and activity inside it. At the same time, the emphasis on descriptive detail allows Hardy to practice something of the concentrated poetic art he loved. Yet his imagination was always attuned to the *adjustment of things unusual to things eternal and universal*,[253] and his melodrama, which often verges on farce or burlesque, has the effect of denaturalizing social life: *distorting* it to bring out the complexities and contradictions of social and sexual power relations by showing *the intense interests, passions, and strategy that throb through the commonest lives*.[254] Hence, Hardy's characters seem plausible and 'rounded' in one light, yet one-dimensional and improbable in other lights; and scenes of poetic density and truthfulness vie for attention with scenes of artificial comedy, broad humour, or operatic absurdity.

*The Woodlanders* is not a pastoral novel, therefore, intent on reconstructing the green world as a refuge from the modern city: *Here, as everywhere, the Unfulfilled Intention, which makes life what it is, was as obvious as it could be among the depraved crowds of a city-slum. The leaf was deformed, the curve was crippled, the taper was interrupted; the lichen ate the vigour of the stalk, and the ivy slowly strangled to death the promising sapling.*[255] Nothing is natural in overcrowded Hintock: the trees are a profitable commodity, the long cycle of their plantation and harvest controlled not by the seasons but by the fluctuations of the timber markets. In similar terms, the novel opens with Barber Percomb persuading Marty South – the country girl whose instinctive knowledge of the woodland and its work-life marks her out as a child of Nature – to sell her hair for an extension for Mrs Charmond. The dissipating metropolitan tendencies of the intruding outsiders only enfeeble an already weakened community. Giles is *autumn's very brother*, whose fate embodies the extinction of the old ways. By an oversight of his own, he is evicted from the cottage in which his family had lived on a copyhold (as the Hardys lived in Bockhampton). For all the *purity of his nature* and ability to read the *hieroglyphs* of the woods as *ordinary writing*,[256] Giles is as vulnerable to the elements as any city-dweller, and, unable to regress to life in his mud hut (again, a Darwinian fossil in the making), he sickens and dies.

In the month *The Woodlanders* came out, Hardy secured a lucrative contract for a new story of the same length with Tillotson and Son, a Lancashire firm run by strict Nonconformists which made its money syndicating fiction to a vast number of regional newspapers.[257] Hardy did not begin work on the new novel – it would become *Tess of the d'Urbervilles* – at once, however. In the spring he and Emma took a much-anticipated trip to Italy, spending a few weeks in Florence, Rome and Venice, where Hardy followed in the footsteps of Shelley and Browning. When they returned to England, he turned his attention to poetry, the ever-evolving Napoleonic epic, and, most immediately, short stories, the writing and publishing of which would parallel his novel writing throughout the 1880s and 1890s.

Robert Browning (1812–89) lived with his wife Elizabeth Barrett in Pisa, Florence and Rome until her death in 1861, when he returned to London. Hardy met him there in the 1880s. Browning's vigorous, dramatic, and strongly visual poems of ideas were important for Hardy, who could not, however, understand how *the smug Christian optimism worthy of a dissenting grocer* could *find a place inside a man who was so vast a seer & feeler.*[258]

There was a large market for popular short fiction in the last quarter of the 19th century, and Hardy produced some 50 stories and sketches of varying lengths over that time. Many of them are hurried and ephemeral, but others – the much anthologized supernatural tale, 'The Withered Arm', for instance, written early in 1888 – are notable achievements in the form. The artistic possibilities of the story sequence began to interest him. He witnessed in Kipling's meteoric ascendancy the enormous potential of the story collection to combine popularity and literary merit – and decided in 1888 to assemble some of his best stories into a volume. In *Wessex Tales*, the imaginary province appears in a title for the first time as a topographic device to unify stories that were published independently as far back as 1879. Over the coming years he would expand his ambitions for Wessex, developing it into a fully mapped region that would overlay his entire creative output.

The rapid rise of the short story after 1880 (and, indeed, its relative unpopularity in our time) was a product of specific social and economic conditions. The achievement of almost universal literacy among English-speaking populations and the greater availability of disposable income produced a spate of cheap magazines and newspapers and a growing demand for fiction to fill their pages. These changing conditions inevitably altered the economic relations between authors and publishers. Mudie and the same small publishing cartel still controlled the production of mainstream fiction (although the three-volume novel was going slowly into decline, and was finally defunct by about 1894), but their influence was beginning to be challenged openly. The Society of Authors was founded by Walter Besant in 1888, and literary agents were increasingly employed to negotiate between authors and publishers. The most visible sign of the shift in author-publisher power relations, however, was the royalty system, which paid authors a percentage of sales instead of a fee in advance. Hardy benefited substantially from these changes, as he did just a few years later when an international copyright agreement finally secured royalties from the spectacularly profitable American market, a development that ultimately freed him to give up fiction altogether – a *trade*, as he later called it, *which he had never wanted to carry on as such.*[259]

That was still some way off, however. In 1888, outdated book-trade practices and the evangelical culture magnates still controlled the production of fiction and continued to impose puritanical restrictions on content. From one point of view, this seemed to be at odds with observable modernizing and liberalizing trends in politics and culture. Gosse's translations of Ibsen; the greater exposure of English readers to progressive French culture (especially the controversial naturalism of Émile Zola and the work of symbolists, aesthetes and decadents such as Huysmans); the suburbanization of aestheticism in design and fashion; the renewed campaign for female suffrage and education for women; the invention of the safety bicycle and its desegregation of the sexes in middle-class leisure pursuits; the popularity of the music-hall, with its risqué material and parading prostitutes: all these developments in different areas of life showed up the timid conservatism of the English novel as a relic of the insular, prudish past.

Perhaps predictably, however, the growing permissiveness of English society provoked a vehement anti-liberal backlash against the various slackenings of moral virtue, and tightly organized conservative social movements campaigned effectively against the threat of French-inspired *fin de siècle* decay. In 1888 concerns were aired in the House of Commons about the spread of demoralizing literature. The National Vigilance Association took action against the London publisher Henry Vizetelly for his translations of Zola and had him imprisoned (the author of the scandalous *Nana* was nevertheless fêted on a subsequent visit to London). There were public outcries – many of them coordinated by the king of populist puritanism, W T Stead, a journalist akin to today's shock-jocks – against white slavery and prostitution. There was a massive and prurient interest in the Whitechapel ('or

The 'New Woman' was a widely disseminated stereotype or ideal of rebellious femininity in the 1890s, thanks to her representation in numerous novels and plays, and in newspapers and magazines – especially by cartoonists. She was typically educated and working, financially independent and happily single, clear-thinking and politically informed, and was often associated with rational dress and cycling.

Jack the Ripper') murders of 1888. Feminists were denounced and the New Woman ridiculed. And, most famously, Oscar Wilde was tried, convicted and jailed for his homosexuality in 1895.

The turbulent climax and abrupt termination of Hardy's career as a novelist later in the decade only makes complete sense if we examine these contradictions, and particularly the violent and shocking brake that the Wilde trials applied to the spirit of permissiveness in England in the 1890s. As the 1890s began, however, Hardy took courage from the brazen outspokenness and irreverence of the Decadents, led by Wilde, Aubrey Beardsley and *The Yellow Book*. The success of *The Woodlanders*, with its daring sidelong treatment of sexual matters, emboldened him. More secure financially and in reputation, he tentatively and with increasing forthrightness began to breathe the energetic anti-establishment atmosphere of Ibsenism, and to speak his mind. The Whistler vs. Ruskin libel trial of 1878 had publicized the new role for art proclaimed by Walter Pater and aestheticism — that it was independent from society, and existed for its own sake — and disclaimed Ruskin's mid-Victorian assertion of the artist's social accountability (and hence moral responsibility). In 1884 the Mudie's three-decker was pilloried as a philistine form (to use Matthew Arnold's famous characterization of the English middle-classes) by George Moore, whose *Literature at Nurse* was written in retaliation against the library's refusal to stock his fiction, and by Gissing, who supported Moore's position in a letter to the *Pall Mall Gazette* in 1884.[260] Hardy's relative eminence encouraged him, too, to voice his displeasure with the system. He did so just as literary culture was starting to free itself up, and just as publishers and moral guardians, on their side, were starting to tighten up in retaliation. He signed the petition protesting against Vizetelly's imprisonment, and in January 1890 was invited to contribute to a *New Review* symposium on 'Candour in English Fiction'. In his response he attacked the magazine and book-lending system for stifling a *conscientious fiction* that *reflected life, revealed life, criticised life*: one *largely concerned with, for one thing, the relations of the sexes.*[261]

Hardy's frustrations with the system came to a head in the protracted sequence of negotiations he went through for *Tess of the d'Urbervilles*. He had begun work on this successor to *The Woodlanders* sometime early in 1889, scouting settings in the dairy country along the valley of the River Frome near Max Gate, and further north in the 'Valley of the Little Dairies' in Blackmore Vale. By mid-July, he had made considerable progress with it and only a few weeks later had gone far enough to sketch out a short summary of the plot and announce its title, 'Too Late, Beloved!': *I can hardly describe the story in brief. The heroine of the narrative is a young country girl, a milkmaid, who is, however, a lineal descendant of one of the oldest county families in the kingdom – of Norman blood and name. But this is only by the way – her personal character & adventures being, of course, the immediate source of such interest as the tale may have. I should say that her position is based on fact.*[262] Half the story was set in type before anyone at Tillotson's actually read what Hardy had written. Shocked by its sensuality and frankness, they politely requested that it 'be recast and certain scenes and incidents deleted entirely'.[263] Hardy stood firm, but Tillotson's could not allow it to proceed unaltered without damaging their relationship with the dozens of regional newspapers they serviced. They graciously agreed to pay out the contracted fee of 1,000 guineas; and Hardy, who was not one to provoke his publishers, equally graciously allowed the contract to be cancelled. It was a wise move. He immediately signed up to supply another serial story to Tillotson's ('The Pursuit of the Well-Beloved').

Having refused to tone down *Tess*, however, Hardy was in a difficult position. He did have a back-up plan: the *Graphic* had been on the lookout for something from him, and they paid well. But he knew they would have the same qualms about the novel because they were just then putting him through the mortifying process of bowdlerizing his latest story sequence, 'A Group of Noble Dames'. He half-heartedly submitted *Tess* to two other magazines to satisfy himself that its sexual censorship was unavoidable (both duly rejected it as unsuitable). Yet he had no intention of sacrificing the two streams of income from magazine serialization and volume publication, and he resigned himself to the dreary routine of removing or changing offending sections for the serial version and replacing them for the book version. This time, however, he hit on the idea of exploiting the potential of this double market. It was *a plan till then, it is believed, unprecedented in the annals of fiction*: to publish it in the *Graphic* as usual *with some chapters or parts of chapters cut out, and instead of destroying these to publish them, or much of them, elsewhere, if practicable, as episodic adventures of anonymous personages.*[264] *Tess* duly appeared in the *Graphic* with some classic Victorian bowdlerization (Angel cannot carry the milkmaids across the flooded lane but must cart them in a wheelbarrow) and without two crucial scenes. In the first, Tess attends a wild country dance and is afterwards raped by Alec in the woods (or seduced: Hardy was more and more vague about what happens in each revision of the novel). For the *Graphic* he had Alec trick Tess into a form of phoney marriage, and adapted the original scene for the chauvinistic and imperialistic Scottish magazine, the *National Observer* (where Tess is transformed into 'Big Beauty', who is *won* by the *masterful, supercilious, coarse* landowner's son). In the second scene, Tess surreptitiously performs a makeshift baptismal ceremony for her dead illegitimate baby, Sorrow, who has been refused a Christian burial. Excised, it appeared in the distinguished radical *Fortnightly Review* (a useful reminder that not *all* Victorian periodicals would have insisted that Hardy clean up *Tess* – but of course the *Observer* and the *Fortnightly* were not high-paying large-circulation magazines like the *Graphic*).

This was a very personal novel for Hardy. He even considered calling it *Tess of the Hardys*, having noticed in his researches around

Blackmore Vale that the *decline and fall of* his own family was *much in evidence*.[265] The novel chronicles more directly than any other the breaking-up of stable rural communities by the enforced traffic of labour up and down the county according to seasonal and market demand. In 'The Dorsetshire Labourer' Hardy had deplored the worst effect of this industrialization of agricultural work: its reduction of individuals and families – those once known intimately by name in the communities where they lived, and whose names had been part of those communities for generations beyond memory – to the nameless 'hodge'. In *Tess* the heroine's *poor wounded name*,[266] Durbeyfield, identifies her as a genetic survival from a long decayed aristocratic family, and her fate becomes tragically bound to the new-moneyed d'Urbervilles, who have randomly appropriated the old name. Hardy is interested in the consequences of this double effacement on a woman. Tess's individuality is effaced by the *family face*, therefore, projecting *trait and trace / Through times to times anon*,[267] and also by the particular anonymity that modern agricultural work imposes on women: *A field-man is a personality afield; a field-woman is a portion of the field; she had somehow lost her own margin, imbibed the essence of her surrounding, and assimilated herself with it*.[268]

*Tess* created a stir by making explicit the connection between economic dependency and sexual exploitation. Hardy openly declared war against the hypocrisy of those who would condemn a good woman for the violence she was forced into by the actions of a sexually predatory man. If Hardy embodies in Alec the gross materialization of love as animal impulses – savagely uninhibited, savagely repressed, and savagely returning – in Angel he represents another kind of exploitation, by a man's over-refined intellectual idealization of the love-object. Tess is 'pure' in that she is the embodiment of Angel's idea of natural womanhood, and therefore unsullied by actuality. Angel is a logical development of the critique of intellectual idealism that Hardy had begun with Knight in *A*

*Pair of Blue Eyes*. When he falls in love with a milkmaid, Angel admires his own daring heterodoxy; but her confession reveals him to be in practice a deeply, instinctually conservative man. With his *fixed, abstracted eyes*, he is another man of mind, like Farfrae, who is attracted to, and an attraction in, the unselfconscious lives of the country folk whose warmth, spontaneity and deeply felt existence he helps to destroy.

*Tess* made Hardy famous overnight and confirmed him with critics as the greatest English novelist since George Eliot – much to Henry James's disgust: 'The good little Thomas Hardy has scored a great success with [*Tess*],' he wrote sourly to Robert Louis Stevenson, 'which is chock-full of faults and falsity and yet has a singular beauty and charm.'[269] The reviews, although mixed, generally (if sometimes grudgingly) acknowledged that it was 'a tragic masterpiece'.[270] Characteristically, though, Hardy was deeply hurt by two notices which explicitly recoiled from the shock of seeing female sexual desire represented: *that tremendous force which sways humanity to its purpose.*[271] One, in the *Saturday Review*, alleged *innuendoes of indecent intentions on my part, which never entered my mind*[272] (referring to Tess's precocious physical development) and took Hardy to task for the poor grammar of what was in fact a misprint. The other, an unsigned notice by Mowbray Morris, who had rejected *Tess* for *Macmillan's Magazine*, sneeringly dismissed it as a 'disagreeable story' told 'in a disagreeable manner', and again criticized Hardy for his voyeurism, suggesting he looked at his heroine like 'a slave-dealer appraising his wares'.[273] *How strange*, he retorted (but only to himself), *that one may write a book without knowing what one puts into it – or rather, the reader reads into it. Well, if this sort of thing continues no more novel-writing for me. A man must be a fool to deliberately stand up to be shot at.*[274]

But the strange power of *Tess* lies in the fact that Hardy really *didn't* know altogether what he'd put into it, for his heroine somehow 'exceeds the boundaries of the language that describes her': he hadn't, he confessed, *been able to put on paper all that she is, or was, to me.*[275] The pointed insinuation in that phrase (he hadn't been able to put it down partly because censorship prevented him) shows how Hardy felt victimized by the same destructive Puritanism that had victimized his heroine. As he revised the novel he made changes which insist on the elusiveness of Tess's nature and the ambiguity of her fate (in this respect she is the opposite of the man of character, Henchard, who suffers for the intransigence of his nature). But his aim was to assert again, this time with the defiant firmness of his subtitle, *A Pure Woman, Faithfully Presented*, that she suffers because ideologies of femininity strive to fix woman *as nature* – as something irreducible and essential (or 'eternal') and something unchanged by culture: something primitive and, at bottom, physiological.

*Tess* divided readers as it did critics. *At dinner parties there was fighting across {the} table over Tess's character*, with one side arguing that she *'deserved hanging. A little harlot!'* and the other defending and pitying her as a *'Poor wronged innocent!'*[276] He was also approached by many of the greatest actresses of the day, including Sarah Bernhardt and Mrs Patrick Campbell, eager to create the role on stage and capitalize on the huge popular outpouring of affection and compassion for Hardy's heroine. Tess captured the public's imagination so powerfully that many readers felt compelled to write to Hardy to tell their own stories and express their devotion to, even their love for, this extraordinarily dignified woman who seemed so much more real than any merely literary character. Such is the intimacy and tenderness that comes through in this novel that readers are left with the strong sense that Hardy had, as he admitted, lost his heart to his heroine.[277] Sublimated, perhaps, in his special fondness for Tess was a growing frustration with his own lost chance of happiness and fulfilment.

Unhappy in marriage, restlessly middle-aged, Hardy found himself more and more attracted to young, beautiful, unattainable women. Some were complete strangers: a prostitute who accosted him in Piccadilly; and women on trains and buses – *a Cleopatra in the railway carriage* with *heavy moist lips*[278] – where daydreams of his early love for his cousin Tryphena Sparks were revived just a few days before he learned, to his shock, of her sudden death in London in March 1890. He tried again and again to find this *lost prize* among all the women he met and befriended through the barren years of his unhappy middle age – all different incarnations of his own melancholy well-beloved. There was nothing exactly lascivious about his attentions, but there is an unmistakable air of sexual and emotional yearning: a frustrated longing for a love relationship with a beautiful, intelligent, receptive woman that is forlornly conscious of its impossibility. This luckless yearning permeates his admiration for the wives and daughters of his friends and acquaintances. He seems to have had a special weakness for their mouths: Agatha Thornycroft, the wife of Gosse's friend Hamo the sculptor, had a mouth *like roses filled with snow* – a simile he also uses for Tess; the novelist 'Lucas Malet' had *a full, slightly voluptuous mouth, red lips, black hair and eyes*.[279] In the mid-1890s he fell in love with Agnes Grove, the daughter of General Pitt-Rivers, and he constantly and unselfconsciously enjoyed the notice of the various daughters of his rich hostesses whose courtships and nuptials he heard all about when he was sat between them at dinner-parties or chatted with them by the fire at country houses. There were, too, much more serious and painful infatuations which Hardy pursued tentatively and with hope, but which ended badly. In the late 1880s he met and fell in love with a talented, aspiring poet named Rosamund Tomson, whose protracted and self-interested flirtation hurt him deeply. He ended their friendship two years later.

In 1892, it seemed the same thing was happening again. In May that year, on a visit to Dublin, he met and fell (this time seriously) in love with the beautiful Florence Henniker – a *charming,* intuitive *woman apparently*, he noted in his diary after that first meeting[280]

Florence Henniker.

– who was, alas, happily married to Lieutenant, later Major-General, Arthur Henniker. Over the following three years Hardy and Mrs Henniker met frequently in London and elsewhere, corresponded regularly, exchanged books and collaborated on a short story, 'The Spectre of the Real'. Hardy's infatuation deepened into love with every meeting, but what to him were romantic assignations were to her only the developing conversation of close friends and fellow writers. Desolated and humiliated by feelings she did not return, he wrote one of the most remarkable accounts of sexual frustration in literature in his new novel (which became *Jude the Obscure*) in the tormented relationship of Jude Fawley and Sue Bridehead, whose middle name is Florence. Mrs Henniker was also the subject of numerous poems which speak of the couple's inevitable division in life and death, and touch with a raw tenderness on the anguish of meeting the unresponsive love-object. Of a broken appointment, the speaker admits to himself at last: you *love not me, / And love alone can lend you loyalty; / I know and knew it.* Of a kept appointment, he remembers bitterly in another poem how the strangers that waited on them mistook them for the lovers they weren't.[281] Yet Hardy and Mrs Henniker remained close friends for 30 years, and Hardy, writing cryptically of the relationship in one of his greatest poems in 1896, suggests why:

*As for one rare fair woman, I am now but a thought of hers,*
*I enter her mind and another thought succeeds me that she prefers;*
*Yet my love for her in its fulness she herself even did not know;*
*Well, time cures hearts of tenderness, and now I can let her go.*[282]

Time had long since cured Hardy's heart of his tenderness for Emma, who was outraged to see her husband's name alongside Florence Henniker's at the head of their collaboration. As the 1890s progressed and Hardy's fame grew, he and Emma drifted further apart. Their friend Sir George Douglas described Emma as a woman 'gifted with spirit and the power of deciding for herself', which had attracted Hardy in his early manhood. She had the makings of a Bathsheba'.[283] There were many times when Hardy had occasion to admire that spirit, as she rose with reckless courage to the defence of working animals (the neglected suffering horses that pulled omnibuses and carriages) and to Hardy's defence too (when she chased off robbers in Italy). But she was also an eccentric, overbearing woman and an aggrieved snob whose sense of the value of her husband's writing was always qualified by the certainty of her own social superiority over him. She had unfulfilled creative aspirations too, and had not been able to share in her husband's writing life in the way she once hoped, and indeed had done in the early years in Cornwall, in Sturminster and during Hardy's illness in Tooting. Locked out from the Max Gate study, subject to Hardy's taciturnity and occasionally irate outbursts, left at home when he visited literary and social acquaintances, and often a source of mute embarrassment to him when visitors were received, Emma progressively retreated into her own private, angry silence, eventually shifting her living quarters up to the attic.

Life at Max Gate had been so difficult for Emma partly because she had no defence against the triumphant clannish Hardys just a mile or two away, especially when the death of Hardy's mild-mannered, appeasing father in 1892 left her to contend with the terrifying Jemima and her husband's sisters alone. Not that they often came face to face: Hardy loyally visited his mother at Bockhampton every Sunday, but Emma and the Hardys conducted sporadic hostilities from a distance. A ferocious letter to Mary, written in 1896, would almost stand as proof of Emma's unhinged mind if its white-hot anger did not ring so true. It accuses Mary of spreading 'evil reports' of her sister-in-law's madness and unkindness to her husband, and strikes back: 'Your brother has been outrageously unkind to me – which is entirely your fault: ever since

I have been his wife you have done all you can to make division between us; also, you have set your family against me ... You are a witch-like creature & quite equal to any amount of evil-wishing & speaking – I can imagine you, & your mother & sister on your native heath raising a storm on Walpurgis night'.[284] There is no evidence, however, that the Hardys' life together was an unrelieved misery. Their childlessness was a mutual unhappiness displaced into a compensatory love for the succession of pets that lay beneath headstones in a ceremonial corner of the Max Gate grounds. And like any settled married couple they were comfortable with each other's habits and foibles, and shared, above all, a common past: something that was extremely important to Hardy, burying as it did the intense love he had once felt for his young wife.

The migrations of love over time were the subject of Hardy's next serial novel for Tillotson's: something light and shorter than usual. It was just the change of pace and mood he needed. *The Pursuit of the Well-Beloved: A Sketch of a Temperament*, begun in December 1891, was deliberately (and ironically) guaranteed by its author to be suitable *for the reading of young people*. He insisted: *There is not a word or scene in the tale which can offend the most fastidious taste*.[285] Nor was it to be *a tragedy in the ordinary sense*, although it is certainly a tragedy of sorts (its sculptor-hero, Jocelyn Pearston, attempts seduction and suicide) even if it may be described more fairly as a return to the comic philosophical romances of the 1880s. *The Pursuit* and its substantially rewritten volume version (simply entitled *The Well-Beloved* and published only in 1897, where the hero is renamed Pierston) are entirely products of their decade – or perhaps, given their important differences, products of those radically different moments in their decade. With their pronounced aestheticism, self-conscious dramatization of a philosophical problem, strikingly novel plot and artificial narrative structure (the hero loves three generations of women in the same family), and their meditation on the relationship between sexual and artistic beauty, *The Pursuit* and *The Well-Beloved* are strongly reminiscent of Oscar Wilde's *The Picture of Dorian Gray*, just out as a volume when Hardy began work on the project. Characteristically, Hardy is more interested than Wilde in the displacement of male heterosexual desire into a disturbing aesthetic idealization and objectification of women (as the *one face with many names* of the novel's epigraph). Yet Wilde read *The Well-Beloved* (in Reading Gaol) and admired it, as Marcel Proust also did.

While *The Pursuit* was appearing in the *Illustrated London News* in 1892 Hardy was planning his next major work of fiction and exploring possible locations in the Oxfordshire countryside of his grandmother Mary Head. He had made notes towards a story about a young man's doomed self-education as early as 1888: *A short story of a young man – 'who could not go to Oxford' – His struggles and ultimate failure.*[286] By early 1893, the outline of *Jude the Obscure* was in place, and writing had begun. Hardy had a contract with the American firm of Harper and Brothers for their family magazine, and once again he insisted that his story *could not offend the most fastidious maiden.*[287] As the writing progressed and the characters developed it became clear that *The Simpletons*, as it was then entitled, was far from suitable. Hardy begged to be released from the contract, and when Harpers refused, he began once again the laborious task of concocting a special serial version.

There is a gaping distance between the overly refined and prettily agitated idealism of Jocelyn Pierston and the shattered ideals of the two chief characters of *Jude the Obscure*, Jude Fawley and Sue Bridehead. Hardy had a peasant's fatalistic fascination with the *something external to us which says 'You shan't!'*,[288] and Sue's despairing protest in the novel recalls all too clearly a note he had made in 1870: *Mother's notion, & also mine: That a figure stands in our van with arm uplifted, to knock us back from any pleasant prospect we indulge in as probable.*[289] But he gradually became more outspoken about what that something external really was: not some universalist fate or vague malign power but real social power, creating sexual hypocrisy, the conventionalism of religious Puritanism, inequality and class prejudice.

Tess Durbeyfield lives and dies in a green world: even the terrible winter in Flintcomb-Ash is a passing blight in a damp and fertile landscape. Jude and Sue, by contrast, are constantly and restlessly on the move through a monotonous brown desert: the vast unhorizoned fields of industrial-scale agriculture; the derelict villages emptied of life; the *decrepit and superseded* medieval buildings of Christminster, a crumbling city with its rotten stones; the dull inns, towns and markets of late-Victorian sepia photographs. In spite of Hardy's claim to the geometric construction of the plot – its familiar pattern of repetitions and doublings – all is turbulence. The novel is, as Hardy explained in the 1912 Preface, just *a series of seemings*, and the arrangement of its parts, 'At Marygreen', 'At Shaston', 'At Christminster' and so on, stresses its terrible perpetual present, where individual growth and historical development are all under siege.

In the 'Preface to the First Edition' Hardy identified the novel's fundamental conflict as *the deadly war waged between flesh and spirit*. Once again, sexual desire is represented candidly as an overpowering drive in both men and women (the pragmatic, sensual Arabella Donn is one of Hardy's most compelling characters). Sexuality collides destructively with the forces of social convention, religiosity, and moral superiority. Jude Fawley is a figure from the familiar territory of Hardy's disempowered agricultural artisan class: a skilled workman who at one point manages to set himself up in business. If he is no representative of the masses, however, Jude nonetheless embodies important stereotypical elements associated with urban working-class masculinity in his uncontrollable passion and the touches of brutishness that he guiltily represses. Jude's own *bodily situation*[290] brings him low. The force of sexual desire, material need, hereditary temperament, sentimental affections, the passion for drink, all conspire against his rarefied intellectual aspirations. At the same time, he and Sue exemplify what for Hardy was a *woeful fact — that the human race is too extremely developed for its corporeal conditions, the nerves being evolved to an activity abnormal in such an environment*.[291] Jude finds in Sue his fatal other half (Hardy is highly conscious of the way Sue is a product of men's imaginations): '*you spirit, you disembodied creature, you dear, sweet, tantalizing phantom — hardly flesh at all*'.[292]

*Jude* has been described as an attempt 'to superimpose the sexual and marital preoccupations of the 1890s upon the intellectual concerns of the 1860s, Hebraism and Hellenism and Mill's liberal individualism'.[293] Its tragedy stems from the ironic displacement of the conventional mid-century story of the pursuit of knowledge under difficulties. In the downward spiralling of Jude's career Hardy rails against the tyranny of social forms — of dead institutions like marriage — and the crushing weight of effort and learning that stands between a working man and his dream of entry into university. But the story also probes the form of the novel itself, finding it inadequate to modern experience. There is no longer any sure story for Jude and Sue: domesticity is no refuge; self-knowledge no compensation. Education itself is reduced to a strained and disoriented set of cultural references and allusions. Jude and Sue assault each other with detached quotations from the great books of Western civilization that do nothing to explain or alleviate their pain.

The uproar from critics and readers of *Jude* broke 'the great silence which immediately followed [the] trial and imprisonment' of Oscar Wilde in July 1895.[294] Hardy had feared for the novel's reception in a culture which he well knew was no longer 'so tolerant of novelty in art and ideas', and his fears were well-founded.[295] *Jude* was a very characteristic product of the 1890s in that it dared to speak *without a mincing of words*[296] about some very sensitive issues. Hardy was irritated that its critics reduced it to a 'novel with a purpose', a disguised polemic against the marriage laws and the protection of privilege by the education system. But *Jude* is unquestionably an angrily didactic and reformist book whose social earnestness is wholly of a piece with the demands for artistic freedom and outspokenness of the Decadent movement. In reviews of the novel Hardy was openly called a decadent – a term of particular opprobrium in that shrinking post-Wildean climate – and a degenerate; and the novel was ceremonially burned by a bishop.

*Jude* came out in book form in November 1895 as part of the first uniform 'collected edition' of Hardy's works: volume vii of 'The Wessex Novels', which he had been preparing for Osgood, McIlvaine and Co whilst working on *Jude*. This first collected edition was a milestone for Hardy. It confirmed his importance as a novelist and gave him an opportunity to revise and reshape his fiction. Much of this revision was topographical, and involved the unification of his fictional world. In the major Preface he added to the revised *Far from the Madding Crowd*, the first volume in the new edition, he wrote: *The series of novels I wrote being mainly of the kind called local, they seemed to require a territorial definition ... to lend unity to their scene. Finding that the area of a single county did not afford a canvas large enough for this purpose, and that there were objections to an invented name, I disinterred the old one*: Wessex.

It is significant that the invention of Wessex and the publication of the handsome collected edition should mark the end of Hardy's career as a novelist: he had arrived. But fame did not abate his anger and indignation. In late 1898 he wrote to a friend: *As to a novel from me, I don't incline to one. Any zest is quenched by the knowledge that by printing a novel which attempts to deal honestly & artistically with the facts of life one stands up to be abused by any scamp who thinks he can advance the sale of his paper by lying about one.*[297] We must remember, too, that when Hardy began publishing fiction in the early 1870s, George Eliot's *Middlemarch* was just appearing and the novel was staking an unlikely claim to be the most prestigious intellectual form in Britain. By the end of the 1890s, only Meredith remained from that distant generation of high-serious Victorians, and the novel had dramatically declined in prestige, returning with a vengeance to its populist roots as a slightly disreputable mass-produced commodity. Hardy was unwilling to put up with the limitations of the commercial market and the hostile protectors of public morals any more. And he didn't have to. The notoriety of *Tess* and *Jude* had assured they were very big sellers, and he could turn his back on the novel a comparatively rich man.

# Poet 1897–1928

Indeed, from another point of view, it might be said that Hardy stopped writing novels much as a successful Victorian professional in late middle-age stopped going to the office every day: not exactly retiring, but content for the business to run itself now that he could afford to pursue passionate interests long neglected. In 1897, he dropped out of the public eye. He joined Emma in the new craze for cycling (through the next decade or more he would venture far afield on his trusty Rover Cob). He assumed greater control of day-to-day household management, to his wife's considerable annoyance, and took a kindly interest in the future of Gordon and Lilian Gifford, Emma's nephew and niece, who frequently stayed with them at Max Gate. He also began preparing a volume of poems for publication. They *were lying about*, he told Gosse with the strained nonchalance of a nervous newcomer, *& I did not quite know what to do with them.*[298]

The volume's title, *Wessex Poems*, and the fact that it was uniform with the 'Wessex Novels' and printed on heavy paper with very wide margins to be as thick as a novel, confirm Hardy's serious intentions for it. At the same time, he decided to illustrate the book with his own drawings, which are naïve in style and amateurish in draughtsmanship, but have a really powerful strangeness about them that adds significantly to the meaning and mystery of the poems they accompany. This decision was prompted, one is tempted to think, by the old *provincialism of feeling*, Hardy's willingness to risk appearing credulous and artless in the honest struggle to make art; and, paradoxically, prompted by his same love of *the art of concealing art*.[299] But it also had the unfortunate effect of encouraging readers to view the verse as the dabbling of a mere amateur. 'What induces Hardy to commit himself to verse!' declared George Meredith (himself a poet turned novelist) in evident horror.

*Wessex Poems* came out in December 1898, and the reviews were at best unenthusiastic, at worst mischievous. The *Saturday*'s unsigned notice was as devastating to the new poet as the *Spectator*'s savaging of *Desperate Remedies* had been to the new novelist nearly 30 years earlier: 'It is impossible to understand why ... [Mr. Hardy] did not himself burn the verse, lest it should ... mar his fame when he was dead.'[300] What most reviewers objected to was the combination of gloomy pessimism and apparent technical incapacity that led to a laboured, unmusical attempt at lyricism.

Percy Bysshe Shelley (1792–1822), educated at Eton and sent down from Oxford for circulating a pamphlet on atheism, was (even more so than his notorious friend, Byron) a symbol among Victorians of the dangerous currents of political radicalism running through Romanticism. He was enormously significant for Hardy, who read him avidly in the 1860s, and drew much from the sustained exploration of idealism in his poetry.

What they didn't acknowledge was that Hardy was no beginner, but had been writing verse since the 1860s (many poems in the volume are dated from that decade). And what they couldn't yet see was that he was a prolific experimenter with traditional poetic forms and techniques. He consciously wrought new effects by yoking together compound words (*heart-halt* and *spirit-lame*), integrating archaic and dialect words, and coining new words from startling conjunctions (*stillicide*) and negatived verbs (*unblooms*). He was also progressive not in turning away from traditional forms but in boldly exploiting their enormous variety, as his great poetic influences, Shelley and

## SHE

### AT HIS FUNERAL

THEY bear him to his resting-place—
   In slow procession sweeping by ;
I follow at a stranger's space ;
His kindred they, his sweetheart I.
Unchanged my gown of garish dye,
Though sable-sad is their attire ;
But they stand round with griefless eye,
Whilst my regret consumes like fire !

187–.

19

'She at His Funeral' from *Wessex Poems* (1898), with illustrations by Hardy himself.

Swinburne, had done, opening them to a new metrical and syntactical ingenuity. Hardy was determined to break new ground with his subject-matter, too, believing that British poetry had degenerated into *the art of saying nothing with mellifluous preciosity.*[301]

    Along with the new freedom to speak, the lyric form demanded a voice at once introspective and public, and Hardy was a famously shy and self-effacing man. In *Jude* he had invested more of himself than ever before. Its distinction as Hardy's last novel – indeed as the exemplar of the last Victorian novel – distracts from its significance as the first book in a new, more confidential phase of his career. Writing in his diary towards the end of 1896, he wondered if he could *express more fully in verse ideas and emotions which run counter to the inert crystallized opinion – hard as a rock – which the vast body of men have vested interests in supporting.*[302] Arguably it was the exposure of his deepest emotions that made the aftermath to *Jude* so painful to him. How could he risk exposing the most private memories, thoughts and feelings in verse? The answer lay in the technicality and heightened artificiality of the form. The discipline of metrical construction, the reliance on metaphor and other poetic figures, and the tendency of Hardy's imagination towards narrative and *dramatic or personative* modes,[303] all provided a buffer between himself and his readers. When he declared, therefore, that *Speaking generally, there is more autobiography in a hundred lines of {his} poetry than in all his novels,*[304] he could do so without the least embarrassment, happily distracting the biography hunters beginning to snoop about in the fiction (and particularly *Jude*) for hidden clues to the author's life.

Nevertheless, in *Wessex Poems* Hardy could look into a mirror and speak candidly about what he saw there:

*I look into my glass,*
*And view my wasting skin,*
*And say, 'Would God it came to pass*
*My heart had shrunk as thin!'*

. . .

*But Time, to make me grieve,*
*Part steals, lets part abide;*
*And shakes this fragile frame at eve*
*With throbbings of noontide.*[305]

This new readiness to write intimately about his own life was understandably distressing to Emma, who felt herself becoming involved in Hardy's public persona in an unexpected, uncomfortable way. Who else could 'The Ivy-Wife' be – she who longed *to love a full-boughed beech / And be as high as he?*[306] Since the treacherous and Godless *Jude* had appeared, Emma was ever more remote and oppositional, living a separate life uncorrupted by her husband's pessimistic view of things and loftily indifferent to his neglect of, and insensitiveness to, her talents and her very different view of the world. Imperiously establishment Anglican, she chose a dogged, combative optimism, and became devoutly evangelical, a fanatically anti-Catholic pamphleteer. Invisible in her cramped quarters in the attic, she wrote devotional poetry, and took up and dropped miscellaneous ultra-conservative and liberal causes, including the women's suffrage movement. At the same time she grew more intransigent and imposing, asserting shrilly her social pre-eminence in front of visitors and guests.

The relative lack of critical interest in *Wessex Poems* did not deter Hardy. There were numberless poems still to be written, some from his fund of old unpublished verses, some from notes going back several decades, and more and more new ones released by the remarkable faculty he had *for burying an emotion in my heart or brain for forty years, and exhuming it at the end of that time as fresh as when interred.*[307] As an example of this faculty, he recorded in his biography the genesis of 'In Time of "The Breaking of Nations"', which famously and economically describes an ancient human landscape: a man and his old horse *harrowing clods*, a smoking heap of couch-grass and a young couple passing by. It ends: *War's annals will cloud into night / Ere their story die.*[308] The poem began, he wrote, in *a feeling that moved me in 1870, during the Franco-Prussian war, when I chanced to be looking at such an agricultural incident in Cornwall. But I did not write the verses till during the war with Germany of 1914.*[309] That the poem's gestation should be bracketed

Hardy (with bicycle), Gordon Gifford and Emma outside Max Gate, 1901.

by two wars is significant, for Hardy found a new career as a public poet given its strongest impetus by outbreaks of war. In October 1899, the British Empire declared war against the independent Boer republics in South Africa, and British troops, including Major Henniker, began embarking from Southampton. Hardy responded to the hostilities with a number of occasional poems, seven of which appeared in newspapers and magazines over the next twelve months. Fascinated since childhood by the romance of the Napoleonic Wars, he admitted that *few persons are more martial than I*.[310] But he was neither jingoist nor imperialist, and abhorred *the fact that 'civilized' nations have not learnt some more excellent & apostolic way of settling disputes than the old & barbarous one*.[311] The war poems reflect those sentiments, deploring the *scheduled slaughter*, and pointing to the irony of another Christmas being celebrated when *the All-Earth-gladdening Law / Of Peace, brought in by that Man Crucified*, has obviously been *ruled to be inept, and set aside*.[312]

The war poems were given pride of place in Hardy's second

collection, *Poems of the Past and Present*, published in November 1901 when the final phase of the Boer War was nearly concluded – pride of place, that is, behind the introductory poem on the death of Queen Victoria, rushed into print in *The Times* only a week after she died on 22 January 1901 and having, as Hardy apologetically put it, *all the crudeness of an unrevised performance*.[313] The bulk of the new volume, however, consisted of 'Miscellaneous Poems', some philosophical and some personal, which are uneven in quality and reveal Hardy's wintry despondency at the end of the Victorian century. Here he is much more direct and probing about the nature of the universe whose indifference had shadowed his fiction: Nature, God, the Absolute – the force that is either *blind, and not a judge of her actions, or … an automaton, and unable to control them*.[314] But this directness can lead to an often tendentious, or at least dryly discursive, unfelt poetry. Elsewhere, there is sometimes a rather glib pessimism, as in 'To an Unborn Pauper Child', and even in the wonderful New Year's Eve anthology-piece, 'The Darkling Thrush', where the speaker sees in the landscape's *sharp features* the *Century's corpse outleant* and wonders how an aged thrush can sing so joyfully: perhaps there is some *blessed Hope, whereof he knew / And I was unaware*.[315] The volume's finest poems – the first of the 'In Tenebris' sequence, 'A Commonplace Day', 'The Self-Unseeing' and 'A Broken Appointment' – are all deeply personal.

It is worth remembering that in the first years of the new century Hardy's innate gloominess was not inconsistent with his faith in human progress, an idea as vital to his mid-Victorian intellectual upbringing as his agnosticism. He remained, in his own mind, hopeful. To the critic William Archer he declared: *my practical philosophy is distinctly meliorist*. War, he was certain, *is doomed. It is doomed* (and here he sounds strangely like George Eliot) *by the gradual growth of the introspective faculty in mankind – of their power of putting themselves in another's place, and taking a point of view that is not their own. What are my books*, he insisted, *but one plea against 'man's inhumanity to man' – to woman – and to the lower animals?*[316] If there is a way forward to *the Better* then *it exacts a full look at the Worst*.[317]

In 1902, when Hardy's contracts with Osgood, McIlvaine expired, he took the opportunity to transfer the rights to Macmillan and Co., for whom he had always had a high regard. The first publishers to receive *The Poor Man and the Lady*, they had encouraged him in the early years, even if they had not always been supportive in their dealings. Now they eagerly took up the rights to the 16 volumes of the 'Wessex Novels', and were true to their promise not to disappoint their famous new client, issuing the completely revised 'Wessex Edition' of the novels, stories and poems in 1912 (the standard edition for many years), and the signed de luxe 'Mellstock Edition' in 1919–20. In 1903, they received the first new work from Hardy, and it was another unexpected change of direction: the long-planned verse drama of the Napoleonic period, *The Dynasts*, the first part of which appeared in January 1904 (the second and third volumes appeared in 1906 and 1908).

*The Dynasts* is the closest Hardy came to writing a philosophical work of art, and he regarded it as the summit of his achievement. It is, however, highly uncharacteristic in its ambitiousness and unity of purpose and its high philosophical seriousness. Hardy was always reluctant to formulate a definitive statement of his ideas because he was convinced of the provisionality of thought and experience, and valued *feelings and fancies*, or *unadjusted impressions* – the *seemings* of *Jude* – over fully developed opinions and certainties.[318] *The Dynasts*, while it is not always consistent, is a serious attempt at a statement of his position, and is the product of an enormous amount of reading and thinking. Here he finally gave a name and a dramatic character to the vague idea of an insensible, amoral *primum mobile* that runs through this later work: the Immanent Will. The epic-drama – it was intended to be read and not performed – is set between the battles of Trafalgar and Waterloo. Its human characters, more than 100 of them, include kings and queens, Napoleon and Pitt, statesmen and aristocrats, soldiers and citizens. Over and above these 'persons', Hardy wrote parts for characterized abstractions, which he called 'Phantom Intelligences': The Ancient Spirit of the Years, The Spirit of the Pities, Spirits Sinister and Ironic, The Spirit of Rumour, and their choruses. Its double view of world-historical events in their immensity and the infinitesimal smallness of their participants, and the dialectic of abstract and human voices, lends *The Dynasts* an air both of grandeur – it is like an ancient epic, an *Iliad of Europe*[319] – and modernity: with its 'panoramic views dissolving into close-up' it looks forward to the large-scale silent cinema of D W Griffith a decade later.[320] Ironically, because his idea of a monumental poetic work comes out of Shelley and the Victorian historical imagination, it is the one poetic work of Hardy's that feels anachronistic and overblown, and for all its uniqueness and experimental daring it is among the least interesting of his great works.

In the course of the five years it took to finish *The Dynasts*, two momentous events occurred. Firstly, Hardy's mother, Jemima, died on Easter Sunday, 3 April 1904, at the age of 90. Despite her advanced age she was as sharp as ever, and Hardy was shocked and devastated by her death. She more than anyone had contributed to the creation of her son's literary kingdom, Wessex; for, as he described her in the *Life*, she was *a woman with an extraordinary store of local memories reaching back to the days when the ancient ballads were everywhere heard … and her good taste in literature was expressed by the books she selected for her children.*[321]

Secondly, in 1905 Hardy met through Mrs Henniker a young school-teacher and writer of children's books, Florence Emily Dugdale, who was 40 years younger than him. Florence was soon established as the amanuensis and friend of both the Hardys, typing and proof-reading Emma's stories and poems, and being taken into her confidence. By 1909, the relationship with Hardy had become more intimate, though the screen of her secretarial assistance allowed it to remain out in the open. Meanwhile, the superior attractions of the far more beautiful Mrs Henniker and Lady Grove faded into the background. Gradually, too, Florence took on the roles that Emma had once dutifully undertaken – of copying passages into notebooks, taking dictation and checking facts. Hardy's study door had long been shut to his wife. He wrote and thought and lived without reference to her, only maintaining the stiff formality of an unhappy marriage which must be endured out a sense of duty, or listlessness. Florence, as the friend of both of them, spent considerable time at Max Gate and witnessed their increasingly violent quarrels. On one occasion she was caught off-balance when Emma invited her to agree that her husband closely resembled Crippen the wife-murderer! But their married life went on as it had, unchanged, for nearly 40 years. With a bleak stubbornness, Hardy was willing to endure what he thought of then as his great mistake without remark, open recrimination or remorse.

When he finished *The Dynasts* in 1907 Hardy felt like *an old Campaigner – just as if I had been present at the Peninsular battles & Waterloo*.[322] He turned 67 in June, but was still as active as ever, overseeing theatrical adaptations of his novels and regularly visiting London for the society, music and theatre. Emma's health was less reliable, and she increasingly cried off the annual relocation for the Season (although she took to disappearing on sporadic jaunts of her own, to Dover and Calais). Hardy did not dissuade her. Fashionable society was moving on, and Hardy's circle of acquaintance contracted to small networks of mostly older intellectual men – many of whom he met through Edward Clodd, the banker and popular anthropologist whose Whitsun house-parties in Aldeburgh were legendary for their gatherings of late-Victorian literary and scientific figures. At this time, too, he met Sydney Cockerell, Director of the Fitzwilliam Museum at Cambridge, who would help arrange for the distribution of his manuscripts to archives, and became his literary executor.

In late 1909, Hardy's next collection of verse, *Time's Laughing-stocks*, appeared. He had proven his worth as a poet of stature with *The Dynasts* (and even the *Saturday* had reluctantly admitted of *Poems of the Past and Present* in 1902 that 'as far as it is possible to be a poet without having a singing voice, Mr Hardy is a poet, and a profoundly interesting one'[323]). But *Time's Laughingstocks* represents a real development, as the sometimes uninspired philosophical poems of the previous collections are subordinated to a moving and original lyric poetry of everyday life, and the often rather tedious ballads of *Wessex Poems* are superseded by the vigorous narrative verse of 'The Trampwoman's Tragedy' and others. Hardy continued the tactic of claiming that the most intimate first-person poems in *Time's Laughingstocks* should be read as *dramatic monologues by different characters*, but that must surely have been to mollify Emma.

The enormity of his life's achievement as a writer, and the culmination of that achievement in *The Dynasts*, were acknowledged in the national, local and academic honours that now flowed to Hardy. In 1908 he declined a knighthood from Asquith's government, to the bitter disappointment of the never-to-be Lady Hardy. In 1910, however, he accepted the more prestigious Order of Merit from George V (it is an honour bestowed personally and infrequently by the sovereign): in June that same year the King had, amusingly, misdirected a telegram of birthday congratulations to the Thomas Hardy who made his fishing rods.[324] He was also given the Freedom of the Borough of Dorchester in 1910, to him the most pleasing of all the honours he received. The literary establishment was less willing to forget the angry dissidence of the 1890s or admit the provincial interloper even in the days of his greatest fame, however, and Hardy was passed over for the post of Poet Laureate in 1913 and never won the Nobel Prize. On

Emma Hardy in 1905.

the other hand, notwithstanding the bitter satire against 'Biblioll College' in *Jude*, Hardy received numerous honorary degrees and university college fellowships. Even when in 1925 he was unable to accept a Litt.D from Bristol in person he received a deputation at Max Gate where the degree was conferred. Edward, Prince of Wales, was only the most distinguished of the pilgrims to the

Hardy and Florence Dugdale on Aldeburgh beach, 1909.

red-brick villa in Dorchester (in 1923); as early as the turn of the century the countryside around Dorchester was regularly invaded by Londoners and overseas visitors making their pilgrimage to Wessex.

Hardy's writing was also slowly beginning to influence a younger generation. The deaths of Swinburne and Meredith in 1909, much regretted by him, left Hardy unchallenged as the foremost English writer of his time, and over the next decade he established new friendships with A E Housman and Siegfried Sassoon. Housman was only 20 years younger than Hardy, but his *A Shropshire Lad*, set in a pastoral 'land of lost content', did not appear until 1896. During the war, in 1916, Sassoon wrote to ask if he might dedicate a volume of poems to Hardy; the two men became close, and Sassoon regularly visited Max Gate over the remaining years of Hardy's life. There were other contacts with the younger 'Georgian poets' too: with Edmund Blunden, who wrote a sympathetic study of Hardy in 1941, Walter de la Mare, and Robert Graves, who recorded his colourful and unreliable recollections of a visit in his autobiography *Goodbye to All That*. D H Lawrence, another onetime Georgian, wrote (but did not publish) a *Study of Thomas Hardy* in 1914 which reveals the enormous debt his radical fiction owed to Hardy's example. Hardy did not expect modernist *vers libre* to survive long in England – or not according to Graves, at least.[325] But while he refused Ezra Pound's invitation to contribute to the progressive *Dial* magazine, Hardy proved an attentive and sympathetic reader of the arch-modernist *Hugh Selwyn Mauberley* (1920).

On the morning of 27 November 1912, Hardy was at work as usual in his study when he was anxiously summoned by Emma's maid to her bedside. She had been sick for days with what he thought was dyspepsia. He had not been up to her rooms for a long time – probably months – and even at this summons, he wasn't persuaded that her condition was serious. He put down his pen, stood up at his desk, and replied to the maid: *Your collar is crooked*. When he arrived at his wife's bedroom door, he found her wracked in pain and unable to speak. She died a few minutes later from a heart seizure. She was 72 years old (it was the day after her birthday), but had been energetic and strong despite the angina from which she had unknowingly suffered.

Given the long unhappiness of his marriage and his long silence about it, Hardy might have been expected to react to her sudden death with ambivalent feelings, and his immediate responsibility for informing her family, organizing the funeral, and deciding where to bury Emma gives us no sense of what he was experiencing. The correspondence that survives from those first few days reflects only the outward formality of grief. The premiere performance of a dramatization of *The Trumpet-Major* had been scheduled in Dorchester on the night of the 27th, and Florence Dugdale and other friends were in town for the occasion. Hardy chose not to cancel this performance, out of courtesy to those who had travelled down, and news of Emma's death was announced from the stage. This distracted gesture was misconstrued as evidence of his indifference.

The true state of Hardy's heart and mind was not apparent to the world at large until the publication in 1914 of his fourth collection of verse, *Satires of Circumstance, Lyrics and Reveries*, which included as a distinct group a set of 18 poems with the unassuming title, 'Poems of 1912–13'. This modest sequence is the series of elegies to Emma which he wrote in the days, weeks and months following her death. The terrible grief which descended upon him out of nowhere released in him a flood of creative activity – more than 50 poems in two years alone – that would only abate with his own death more than a decade and a half, and hundreds of poems, later.

'Poems of 1912–13' is structured, like the other earlier elegies to which it refers – via Coventry Patmore's *The Unknown Eros* (written in 1877), to Tennyson's *In Memoriam* (of 1850), back to Shelley's *Adonais* (of 1820), and thence to Milton's *Lycidas* (of 1637) – on a pattern of successive stages: what Freud called 'the work of mourning', in which the death of the beloved triggers shock, disbelief, and anguish, and breeds a pervasive, insidious despair, as if the senselessness and ghastliness of existence were suddenly revealed to the bereaved. Only a form of visionary confrontation or union with the beloved can bestow the gift of consolation and restore meaningfulness. Traditionally, the elegy appeals to the great – the virtually transcendent – spiritual authority of its subject, and through them to the acknowledgement of a universal Godhead. Edward King in *Lycidas*, John Keats in *Adonais* and Arthur Hallam in *In Memoriam* may not (or not yet) be public figures when they die, but they loom as inspirations above the poets who mourn them: they are figures fit to carry the public struggles with belief and meaning that their deaths and elegies occasion. In

'Poems of 1912–13' Hardy does something different, something new. He writes an elegy to an undistinguished, unknown individual, who is important only to him. And he writes, for the first time, the elegy of an unbeliever. Exploiting the elegiac tradition in which he is working, Hardy is able to draw from these deeply personal and painful meditations on Emma's death something strikingly modern: 'Poems of 1912–13' is the anatomy of a grief experienced and survived in a world without God.

The shape of the 'Poems of 1912–13' originates in two discoveries Hardy made when he was going through his wife's belongings in the attic rooms immediately after her death. One was a secret journal of recriminations which she had kept for some ten years, ominously entitled 'What I Think of my Husband'. The other was a series of personal reminiscences of her girlhood, 'Some Recollections', written only in the previous year. The secret diary shocked him, and he destroyed it almost immediately, putting its obsessiveness and paranoia down to his wife's late mental instability. But he could not erase what it so starkly told him: of the years of bitterness and withdrawal, and the lovelessness of their lives. The manuscript of 'Some Recollections', on the other hand, which traced Emma's passionate early love for the man she married, the man who was irrevocably changed, sent him back to the days of their courtship in Cornwall in the early 1870s, and brought back with surprising intensity what Hardy had found so attractive about her in those days: the independent horsewoman ranging over the hills and cliffs, the couple washing their hands together in a waterfall, or looking out over Pentargan Bay. These two documents set the parameters of the 'Poems of 1912–13': Dorset and Cornwall, the loveless marriage and loving courtship, the unbearable present and the longing for the past.

The sequence is accordingly divided into two parts: Dorset poems take up most of the first half, and Cornwall poems dominate the second half (though the sequence does finally return to Dorset).

At home, left behind by the woman who never said goodbye, the woman whom he ignored and took for granted for so long, Hardy searches out Emma's fugitive image and voice, questioning her in a tone which is at once anxious and mildly rebuking:

> *Why did you give no hint that night*
> *That quickly after the morrow's dawn,*
> *And calmly, as if indifferent quite,*
> *You would close your term here, up and be gone*
>     *Where I could not follow*
>     *With wing of swallow*
> *To gain one glimpse of you ever anon!*[326]

This poem lays out the central concerns of the sequence: indifference – the indifference of the dead and the inanimate world, the overwhelming sense of 'unknowing'; the wish for a word, when all has been silence, and now it is too late to speak; and the striving for *time's renewal* when it is too late for the renewal of love. In the end the poet remains stranded in his empty present, still more or less *the dead man held on end* of the opening lyric.[327] He reaches a degree of acceptance and comprehension, but well knows at last, as many of the speakers in Hardy's poems do, that he has discovered what is most important to him only when it is too late to act upon the discovery. Consciousness is no solace, but an intolerable burden for the living left behind. For only before life and after life does all go well: to await wellbeing is to await death.

In the 'Poems of 1912–13' Hardy found himself surprisingly at ease with a poetry that spoke plainly and unflatteringly in public about his own dismal marriage, its incandescent and erotic beginnings, its long, unhappy decline, and its poignant aftermath. The idea of including such poems in *Satires of Circumstance* was, he mused to the Cambridge don A C Benson, both *indecent* and *quite natural: very intimate, of course – but the verses came.*[328] In his next volume, he would make more of this lyric freedom he had discovered, opening his art to a flood of memories, visions, impressions, and ideas that would encompass his whole life. *Moments of Vision and Miscellaneous Verses* (1917) is generally agreed to be Hardy's greatest volume of poems. It had its origins in the period of prolonged personal suffering that began with Emma's death and reached its crisis in 1915, during the darkest days of the Great War, when death seemed to be closing over him. That year he lost his beloved sister, Mary, and his favourite cousin and chosen heir, Frank George (in the fighting at Gallipoli). This war to end all wars summarily terminated his circumspect faith in the evolutionary betterment of humanity. Now, he frankly feared the destruction of civilization. But at 75 he was more energetic than ever, writing out of his despair in a white heat as he had in 1912–13, drawing on the vivid, irrepressible memories and daydreams with which he was continuously assaulted. Almost all of the poems in *Moments of Vision* – a book *rather in keeping*, he admitted, with the *wars & tumults* that attended its publication[329] – were written between 1913 and 1916, and most of them in 1915 or after.[330]

Still unable to recover fully from the acute guilt and grief brought on by Emma's death, Hardy was by this time increasingly unwell himself, and still childless whatever hopes he may have held for his new life with Florence, whom he married in the parish church at Enfield near her family home on 10 February 1914. Inevitably, it seemed: since Emma's death, Florence had virtually run the Max Gate household – though how she must have had to endure her new husband's astonishing grief and remorse-ridden change of heart! – and was utterly indispensable to Hardy. It was probably only because of her reassuring presence that he was ever able to contemplate seriously Sydney Cockerell's request in 1915 that he write something down about himself, 'and especially about that youthful figure ... of whom you told me you could think with almost complete detachment'.[331] Hardy was not temperamentally

The Prince of Wales visiting Hardy and his second wife Florence at Max Gate in 1923.

attracted to the project, but he dreaded, Florence wrote, 'the person who comes here & goes away to write down things': autograph hunters, journalists and interviewers, academics, even friends.[332] In January 1916 he learned that his old friend Edward Clodd intended publishing his memoirs. According to Florence – she was herself a rich source of news and gossip from Max Gate[333] – Hardy was horrified at this prospect. He had believed Clodd 'would be perfectly safe – a man whom he trusted implicitly', but 'Now he finds that he has been keeping a record of all conversations etc – & they will probably be published. Two other men of his acquaintance (friends I might say) also keep diaries & it is generally supposed that they will publish their reminiscences too'.[334] Hardy's fears were unfounded. But as he retreated farther and farther out of 'the active world',[335] the active world came in pursuit of him, and he was passionately determined to protect his privacy. The publication of a biographical chapter in a study by F A Hedgcock in Paris in 1911, *Thomas Hardy: penseur et artiste*, enraged him with its impertinence, inaccuracy and invasiveness, and with its persistent refusal – the refusal of so many readers and commentators – to recognize 'the *key* to the books – i.e. the verse'.[336]

Although a constitutionally backward-looking man, Hardy's mood was so intensely introspective that the idea of publishing his own memoirs must have seemed a trivial distraction – an occupation for retired bankers – especially when his poetic imagination was being so vigorously renewed by these onslaughts of personal sorrow, age, and cultural despair. He did not actively pursue his reminiscences, therefore, until the *Moments of Vision* manuscript was virtually finished, in the first half of 1917. An 18-page typescript headed 'Notes of Thomas Hardy's Life./ by Florence Hardy. / (taken down in conversations etc.)'[337] was completed by December 1917. This was something of a preliminary or pilot undertaking, aimed at finding the most effective working methods for the project.[338] Once those methods were established, by early 1918, Hardy and Florence worked steadily together for more than two years. The *Life* was substantially finished by mid-1920, although Hardy went on revising and adding to it through the remaining years of his life.

Hardy published three further volumes of verse after *Moments of Vision*: *Late Lyrics and Earlier* (1922), *Human Shows, Far Phantasies, Songs and Trifles* (1925), and the posthumous *Winter Words in Various Moods and Metres* (1928), as well as a *Selected Poems* in 1916 and another verse-drama, *The Famous Tragedy of the Queen of Cornwall* in 1923. His total verse output amounted to something like 1,000 poems, without, remarkably, any deterioration in quality. Hardy continued to pull old poems out of his bottom drawer, some of them from the 1860s, and to go on writing new ones with the same energy and inventiveness, publishing many of them first in newspapers and periodicals.

Hardy's coffin leaving Max Gate after his death on 11 January 1928.

On 11 December 1927, Hardy sat down at his desk as usual but could write nothing. He went back to bed and more or less stayed there, gradually losing his strength and some alertness. Over the few next weeks, his mind reverted to Emma and the terrible sorrow, and as death approached, he went though his own last rites. He dictated two spleenful epitaphs against personal slights by the writers G K Chesterton and George Moore (probably remembering Moore's prediction that his low opinion of Hardy's botched and bungled writing would become the general opinion when the author 'steps on board Charon's boat'[339]). He asked for a rasher of bacon to be cooked on the open fire in the old way, and called for Florence to read from the *Rubaiyat of Omar Khayyam*. She and her sister Eva, a qualified nurse, were the only ones in the sickroom when, on the evening of 11 January 1928, Hardy suffered a massive heart attack. Minutes later, as a look of horror crossed his face, he cried out *Eva, what is this?* and died.

Even in death Hardy was a divided man. His will stipulated that he should lie where he and generations of his family had been born and christened and buried, in the churchyard at Stinsford – Mellstock, the imaginative heart of his own Wessex – where Emma was, and Thomas and Jemima, and his grandparents. But Cockerell and Barrie had other ideas, which Hardy may not entirely have disapproved of. It was decided, rather grotesquely and hurriedly, that his heart should be cut out and buried at Stinsford, and his remains cremated and entombed in Poet's Corner in Westminster Abbey. This honour was a testament to the extraordinary renown in which he was held – he lies alongside Chaucer and Spenser, Dickens and Tennyson: a provincial boy, an agnostic of all things, admitted to that temple of the social and religious establishment. At the two services, one in the bleak London winter where the prime minister and opposition leader were pallbearers, the other beneath the cold blue sky in Stinsford, Thomas Hardy resolved to say no more:

> *if my vision range beyond*
> *The blinkered sight of souls in bond,*
> *   – By truth made free –*
> *   I'll let all be,*
> *And show to no man what I see.*[340]

# Afterwards

In the Dorset County Museum there is a large display case filled with the tools and ceremonial objects of a writer's life. It is also an empty room: Hardy's Max Gate study. Relocated piece by piece, it is eerily realistic behind its darkened glass partition. The cardinal-red walls and cream cornices and skirting boards; the modest, elegant coal fireplace; the small framed engravings from the novels: everything is authentic. Bookcases are neatly ranged with Hardy's own books, including a set of the Mellstock Edition with its few lightly pencilled holograph corrections on the inside covers. A violin and a cello from the days of the Stinsford choir sit and stand in their old places in silence. The brightly upholstered chairs seem never to have been sat in, and the desk is tidy and dustless with its blotter, ink bottle and paper at the ready. And one other thing – the desk calendar, fixed permanently by Hardy on 7 March 1870: the date he met Emma Lavinia Gifford in St Juliot in Cornwall.

It is ironic, or perhaps only fitting, that this room, where Hardy shut the door on everyone for days, weeks, months on end, should fix our image of the uneventful, necessarily selfish writer's life. We are not invited in, and peer helplessly through the glass, straining to imagine the absent great man thinking and working here. Yet right outside the doors of the museum another exhibition space is spread out democratically before us: the 'Hardy country', where we are promised a more intimate and involving experience. This

Hardy's desk in the Dorset County Museum.

open-air theme park, Wessex, began to take shape in Hardy's lifetime. The first magazine article to recommend using the fiction as an informal touring guide to Dorset appeared as early as 1891, before the *partly real, partly dream-country* was formalized and authorized by Hardy in the 'Wessex Novels'.[341] This visitable Wessex began to take on a different sort of life in the real places that were its inspiration, and its creator was diligent in encouraging sales of his work but dismayed to think of its creative control passing to the readers who were so eager to anticipate him in making maps and writing guidebooks, and turning up on his doorstep to join him in walking and photographing the scenery of the novels.

There is something about Hardy's writing and its many screen versions that impels readers and viewers to see the scenes for themselves, and Wessex remains one of the most popular literary tourism regions in the world. Is it because the tourism industry and the media have reduced Wessex to an empty spectacle, where we make no real contact with the people who live there or once lived there? The orthodox critical view of Hardy tourism has generally dismissed the 'Wessex Worshippers' as idle holiday-makers, who have 'shaped their own version of Wessex and made it into a mythic image for England itself', thereby reducing 'Hardy's complex and realistic fiction ... to a one-dimensional, repetitious chronicle of an appealingly timeless and nonmaterial way of life under siege'.[342] From this point of view, the tourist Wessex smoothes out 'Hardy's fiction, with its complicated and tense relations with modernity and shockingly progressive views' into a 'record of heart-warming and wholesome rural authenticity'.[343] Or, it thrives because of a continuing need to maintain a cohesive national consciousness by promoting the 'myth of a rural national past'.[344] The tourist who is assumed to be the principal carrier of this powerful myth is also the uneducated reader who privileges rural pastoralism, tragic realism and a misguided belief in the 'reality' of Hardy's world.

Yet there has been little or no attempt to understand what visitors to Wessex actually come in search of, and whether they find it; nor to acknowledge that tourism has been vital to the development of Hardy criticism as well as the Dorset economy. As we have seen from his own life, the two dominant images of Hardy, one the province of amateur reader-tourists and the other of professional Hardyans, are not in fact contradictory. His own unresolvable social dislocation gave him a profound and unique insight into what he called the *ache of modernism*.[345] When he realized after a decade of struggle that it was impossible to conceal his provincialism or sell himself as a novelist of metropolitan manners, he resolved to turn the entire game on its head, setting up openly as a regionalist at Max Gate whose defiantly local writing would speak more eloquently about modernization – 'a process by which capitalism uproots and makes mobile that which is grounded'[346] – than any urban fiction did. He could do so because he too had lost his place and, uprooted and ungrounded, relied on the power of his imagination to reconnect meaningfully and without nostalgia with where he was and where he had come from. Hardy was an outsider in his own countryside, yet the detachment of his perception of it was never incompatible with the passionate, loving attention he brought to it. Tourists do not always visit this Wessex, then, in order to consume a recreated traditionalism. They find there instead a place which reminds them that they have *lost touch with their environment, and that sense of long local participancy*,[347] and are inspired by Hardy's example to a truer *art of observation ...: the seeing of great things in little things.*[348] We become, as he was, noticers for the first time, in the selfsame ancient landscape that is astir with the present, and the noise from the nearby A35, and the traffic that clogs the Dorchester High Street all the way to Grey's Bridge at the bottom.[349]

# Notes

1. Virginia Woolf, 'The Novels of Thomas Hardy', *The Common Reader: First and Second Series* (Harcourt Brace, New York: 1948) p 266.

2. Thomas Hardy, 'Preface' to *Far from the Madding Crowd*, in *Thomas Hardy's Personal Writings*, ed Harold Orel (Macmillan, London: 1966) p 9, hereafter *Personal Writings*.

3. Thomas Hardy, 'General Preface to the Wessex Edition of 1912' in *Personal Writings*, p 46.

4. A detailed account of the events leading up to the erection of the memorial is given in Michael Millgate, *Testamentary Acts: Browning, Tennyson, James, Hardy* (Clarendon Press, Oxford: 1992) pp 147–52.

5. Quoted in Raymond Williams, *The Country and the City* (Chatto and Windus, London: 1973) p 199.

6. Sven Birkerts, *The Gutenberg Elegies: The Fate of Reading in an Electronic Age* (Fawcett Columbine, New York: 1994) p 25.

7. Birkerts, *The Gutenberg Elegies*, p 27.

8. Thomas Hardy, 'Preface' to *Jude the Obscure*, and 'Preface' to *Far from the Madding Crowd*, in *Personal Writings*, pp 3, 9.

9. Christopher C Taylor, *Dorset. The Making of the English Landscape* (Hodder & Stoughton, London: 1970) p 29.

10. Thomas Hardy, 'In Time of "The Breaking of Nations"' in *The Complete Poems*, ed James Gibson (Macmillan, London: 1976) p 543, hereafter *Complete Poems*.

11. Williams, *The Country and the City*, p 197.

12. Peter Widdowson, 'Hardy in History' in Widdowson, *On Thomas Hardy: Late Essays and Earlier* (Macmillan, London: 1998), p 34. See also Widdowson's full-length *Hardy in History: A Study in Literary Sociology* (Routledge, London: 1989).

13. Thomas Hardy, 'General Preface to the Wessex Edition of 1912' in *Personal Writings*, p 46.

14. Widdowson, 'Hardy in History', p 43.

15. Thomas Hardy, *The Woodlanders*, ed Patricia Ingham (Penguin, London: 1998) p 8.

16. Florence Emily Hardy, *The Early Life of Thomas Hardy, 1840–1891* (Macmillan, London: 1928) p 82, hereafter *Early Life*.

17. Thomas Hardy, 'On Receiving the Freedom of the Borough' in *Thomas Hardy's Public Voice: The Essays, Speeches and Miscellaneous Prose*, ed Michael Millgate (Clarendon Press, Oxford: 2001) p 322, hereafter *Public Voice*.

18. George Gissing, in James Gibson (ed), *Thomas Hardy: Interviews and Recollections* (Macmillan, Basingstoke: 1999) p 50, hereafter Gibson (ed), *Interviews and Recollections*.

19. 'Celebrities at Home: Mr. Thomas Hardy at Max Gate, Dorchester', *World* (Feb 1886) pp 6–7, in Gibson (ed), *Interviews and Recollections*, p 21.

20. Ford Madox Ford, in Gibson (ed), *Interviews and Recollections*, p 30.

21. Ford Madox Ford, in Gibson (ed), *Interviews and Recollections*, p 30.

22. Leslie Ward, *Forty Years of 'Spy'* (Chatto and Windus, London: 1915) p 291.

23. Ward, *Forty Years of 'Spy'*, p 291.

24. Edmund Gosse, quoted in Ann Thwaite, *Edmund Gosse: A Literary Landscape, 1849–1928* (Oxford University Press, Oxford: 1985) p 507.

25. Brooke, in Gibson (ed), *Interviews and Recollections*, p 82.

26. T P O'Connor, in Gibson (ed), *Interviews and Recollections*, p 26.

27. George Gissing, in Gibson (ed), *Interviews and Recollections*, p 50.

28. Edith Wharton, *A Backward Glance* (D Appleton-Century Co., New York: 1934) p 216.

29. Brooke, in Gibson (ed), *Interviews and Recollections*, p 82.

30. *Early Life*, p 301.

31. Thomas Hardy, 'So Various', in *Complete Poems*, pp 870–1.

32. Thomas Hardy, *The Literary Notebooks of Thomas Hardy*, ed Lennart Bjork, 2 vols (Macmillan, London: 1985) vol 1, p 165 (n 1352), hereafter *Literary Notebooks*.

33. F R Leavis, *New Bearings in English Poetry* (1932; Penguin, Harmondsworth: 1963) p 53.

34. *Early Life*, p 3.

35. *Early Life*, p 18.

36. *Early Life*, p 18. Hardy inserted this episode into the manuscript of Chapter 5 of *The Later Years of Thomas Hardy 1892–1928*. It was moved into *Early Life*, slightly reworded, by Florence Hardy.

37. *Early Life*, p 42.

38. Thomas Hardy, *The Collected Letters of Thomas Hardy*, ed Richard L Purdy and Michael Millgate, 7 vols (Clarendon Press, Oxford: 1978–88) vol 1, p 89, hereafter *Collected Letters*.

39. *Early Life*, p 5.

40. For example, in Robert Gittings, *Young Thomas Hardy* (Heinemann, London: 1975).

41. *Early Life*, p 9.

42. Thomas Hardy, 'One We Knew', in *Complete Poems*, pp 274–5.

43. Thomas Hardy, *The Woodlanders*, ed Patricia Ingham (Penguin, London: 1998) p 125.

44. T E Lawrence, *The Letters of T E Lawrence*, ed D Garnett (Jonathan Cape, London: 1938) p 429.

45. Thomas Hardy, 'One We Knew', in *Complete Poems*, pp 274–5.

46. *Early Life*, p 16.

47. *Early Life*, p 18.

48. *Early Life*, p 18.

49. *Early Life*, pp 26–7.

50. *Early Life*, p 20.

51. Thomas Hardy, 'So Various', in *Complete Poems*, pp 870–1.

52. *Early Life*, p 27.

53. Hardy described himself 'beset' by scenes in 'In Front of the Landscape', in *Complete Poems*, pp 303–5.

54. *Collected Letters*, vol 7, p 5.

55. *Early Life*, p 10.

56. *Early Life*, p 26.

57. Thomas Hardy, *Tess of the D'Urbervilles*, ed Tim Dolin (Penguin, London: 1998) p 23, hereafter *Tess of the D'Urbervilles*.

58. *Early Life*, p 265.

59. *Early Life*, p 20.

60. *Early Life*, p 23.

61. *Early Life*, pp 24, 25.

62. *Early Life*, p 134.

63. Thomas Hardy, 'Preface' to *A Pair of Blue Eyes*, in *Personal Writings*, p 7.

64. Thomas Hardy, *The Mayor of Casterbridge*, ed Keith Wilson (Penguin, London: 1997) p 322. See Pamela Dalziel, 'The

Gospel According to Hardy', in *Thomas Hardy Reappraised: Essays in Honour of Michael Millgate*, ed Keith Wilson (University of Toronto Press, Toronto: 2006) pp 3–19.

65. Bastow became the Victorian Department of Works's head architect to the Education Department from 1873. He died in 1920. See Lawrence Burchell, *Victorian Schools: A Study in Colonial Government Architecture 1837–1900* (Melbourne University Press, Carlton: 1980).

66. See Patricia Ingham, 'Hardy and *The Wonders of Geology*', *Review of English Studies*, 31 (Feb 1980) pp 59–64.

67. Charles Taylor, *Sources of the Self: The Making of the Modern Identity* (Cambridge University Press, Cambridge: 1989) p 404.

68. Thomas Hardy, *A Pair of Blue Eyes*, ed Pamela Dalziel (Penguin, London: 1998) p 94. This edition uses the text of the 1873 first edition. Hardy moderated his opinion of Stephen in later editions. Stephen, like Tolbort, goes to India in the novel.

69. Thomas Hardy, *Jude the Obscure*, ed Dennis Taylor (Penguin, London: 1998) p 182.

70. According to the 1861 Census.

71. *Early Life*, p 54.

72. *Early Life*, p 55.

73. *Early Life*, p 48.

74. *Early Life*, p 59.

75. *Early Life*, p 49.

76. *Early Life*, p 58.

77. *Early Life*, pp 58–9.

78. John Britton and Augustus Charles Pugin, quoted in B Kaye, *The Development of the Architectural Profession in England. A Sociological Study* (George Allen & Unwin, London: 1960) p 117.

79. *Early Life*, p 61.

80. *Early Life*, p 61.

81. The career of Walter Tapper (1861–1935), who was, like Hardy, born in an obscure rural family in the building trade, demonstrates how rarely poor men to made it to the top of the architectural profession. Tapper trained and worked as an assistant before going out on his own at age of 40. He became president of the RIBA, and was knighted in the year of his death.

82. Thomas Hardy, *Thomas Hardy's Studies, Specimens &c. Notebook*, ed Pamela Dalziel and Michael Millgate (Clarendon Press, Oxford: 1994) pp 59, 89.

83. Horace Moule, Letter to Thomas Hardy, 21 Feb 1864 (Dorset County Museum).

84. *Early Life*, p 62.

85. It appeared in the issue of 18 March 1865.

86. *Early Life*, p 62.

87. See Thomas Hardy, 'Schools of Painting Notebook', in *The Personal Notebooks of Thomas Hardy*, ed Richard H Taylor (Macmillan, London: 1979) pp 103–14, hereafter *Personal Notebooks*, and J B Bullen, *The Expressive Eye: Fiction and Perception in the Work of Thomas Hardy* (Clarendon Press, Oxford: 1986).

88. *Early Life*, p 62.

89. *Collected Letters*, vol 5, p 174. See Ralph W V Elliott, *Thomas Hardy's English* (Oxford, Basil Blackwell: 1984) pp 120–6.

90. *Early Life*, p 69.

91. In V S Pritchett, *George Meredith and English Comedy* (Chatto and Windus, London: 1970).

92. *Early Life*, p 72.

93. Thomas Hardy, *Studies, Specimens &c. Notebook*, p 61.

94. See *Meredith: The Critical Heritage* ed Ioan Williams (Routledge and Kegan Paul, London: 1971) pp 92–107.

95. Thomas Hardy, 'She, to Him, II', in *Complete Poems*, p 15.

96. Thomas Hardy, 'Neutral Tones', in *Complete Poems*, p 12.

97. Thomas Hardy, 'Hap', in *Complete Poems*, p 9.

98. Thomas Hardy, 'At a Bridal', in *Complete Poems*, p 10; *Early Life*, p 66.

99. Written in response to an attack by Charles Kingsley, Newman's *Apologia pro Vita Sua* (i.e. a defence of one's life) was the most important spiritual autobiography of the age of doubt.

100. Florence removed the passage from the *Life*. It may be read in the Hardy-only edition of the work: Thomas Hardy, *The Life and Work of Thomas Hardy*, ed Michael Millgate (Macmillan, London: 1984) p 51.

101. *Early Life*, p 66.

102. *Literary Notebooks*, vol 1, pp 5, 6 (nn 2, 13).

103. *Early Life*, p 66.

104. *Literary Notebooks*, vol 1, pp 5 (n 8).

105. Thomas Hardy, *The Later Years of Thomas Hardy, 1892–1928* (Macmillan, London: 1930) p 119, hereafter *Later Years*.

106. *Later Years*, p 119.

107. *Early Life*, p 76.

108. *Early Life*, p 70.

109. *Early Life*, p 74.

110. *Early Life*, p 64.

111. *Early Life*, p 70.

112. *Early Life*, p 74.

113. *Early Life*, p 74.

114. Arthur Quiller-Couch, *The Art of Writing* (Guild Books, London: 1946) p 33.

115. *Early Life*, p 75.

116. *Early Life*, p 79.

117. *Early Life*, p 64.

118. *Early Life*, p 53.

119. *Early Life*, pp 77–8.

120. *Early Life*, p 81.

121. *Early Life*, p 81.

122. Quoted in Michael Millgate, *Thomas Hardy: A Biography Revisited* (Oxford University Press, Oxford: 2004) pp 102–3.

123. *Collected Letters*, vol 1, p 8.

124. *Early Life*, p 82.

125. Thomas Hardy, 'Thoughts of Phena: At News of her Death', in *Complete Poems*, p 62. On the biographical controversy over Tryphena Sparks see the Appendix 'Hardy and Tryphena Sparks' in Gittings, *Young Thomas Hardy*.

126. Emma Hardy, from 'Some Recollections', in *Early Life*, p 89.

127. Emma Hardy in *Early Life*, p 92.

128. Emma Hardy in *Early Life*, p 89.

129. Emma Hardy in *Early Life*, p 90.

130. Emma Hardy in *Early Life*, p 91.

131. Thomas Hardy, 'Beeny Cliff', in *Complete Poems*, p 350.

132. Emma Hardy in *Early Life*, pp 93–4.

133. Thomas Hardy, 'A Dream or No', in *Complete Poems*, p 348.

134. Emma Lavinia Hardy and Florence Emily Hardy, *Letters of Emma and Florence Hardy*, ed Michael Millgate (Clarendon Press, London: 1996) p 3, hereafter *Letters of Emma and Florence Hardy*.

135. Quoted in Millgate, *Thomas Hardy: A Biography Revisited*, pp 116–17.

136. *Early Life*, p 112.

137. Unsigned Review of *Desperate Remedies*, *Spectator* (22 Apr 1871), in *Thomas Hardy: The Critical Heritage*, ed R G Cox (Routledge and Kegan Paul, London: 1970) p 3, hereafter *Critical Heritage*.

138. *Collected Letters*, vol 1, pp 13–14.

139. *Collected Letters*, vol 1, p 16.

140. *Collected Letters*, vol 1, p 17.

141. Horace Moule to Thomas Hardy, 21 May 1873 (undated letter, Dorset County Museum).

142. *Early Life*, p 125.

143. *Early Life*, p 132.

144. *Early Life*, p 131.

145. *Early Life*, p 126.

146. *Early Life*, p 127.

147. *Early Life*, p 127.

148. Thomas Hardy, *The Hand of Ethelberta*, ed Tim Dolin (Penguin, London: 1996) p 312.

149. *Early Life*, p 129.

150. *Personal Notebooks*, p 17.

151. *Early Life*, p 288.

152. *Collected Letters*, vol 3, p 218.

153. Emma Hardy, *Some Recollections*, ed Evelyn Hardy and Robert Gittings (Oxford University Press, Oxford, 1979) p 60.

154. *Early Life*, p 129.

155. *Early Life*, p 85.

156. *Early Life*, p 134.

157. *Early Life*, p 136.

158. *Early Life*, p 135.

159. *Early Life*, p 137.

160. *Early Life*, p 138.

161. Henry James, Review of *Far from the Madding Crowd*, *Nation* (24 Dec 1874), in *Critical Heritage*, pp 28, 31.

162. *Early Life*, p 277.

163. *Collected Letters*, vol 1, p 262.

164. *Early Life*, p 189.

165. *Early Life*, p 279.

166. Lytton Strachey, Review of *Satires of Circumstance*, *New Statesman* (23 Dec 1914), in *Critical Heritage*, p 437.

167. *Early Life*, p 143; F W Maitland, *The Life and Letters of Leslie Stephen* (Duckworth, London: 1906) p 450.

168. *Early Life*, p 135.

169. Thomas Hardy, 'We sat at the Window', *Complete Poems*, p 429.

170. Emma Hardy, *Emma Hardy Diaries*, ed Richard H Taylor (Mid-Northumberland Arts Group, Ashington: 1985) p 103.

171. Thomas Hardy, 'A Two-Years' Idyll', in *Complete Poems*, pp 628–9.

172. *Early Life*, p 153.

173. *Early Life,* p 156.

174. Thomas Hardy, *Tess of the D'Urbervilles*, ed Tim Dolin (Penguin, London: 1998) p 118.

175. Thomas Hardy, 'Candour in English Fiction', in *Personal Writings*, p 127.

176. See Peter Widdowson, 'Thomas Hardy at the End of Two Centuries: From page to Screen', in *Thomas Hardy and Contemporary Literary Studies*, ed Tim Dolin and Peter Widdowson (Palgrave Macmillan, Basingstoke: 2004) pp 178–98 and especially pp 182–4.

177. *Early Life*, p 282. *All comedy is tragedy, if you only look deep enough into it*: *Collected Letters*, vol 1, p 190.

178. *Later Years*, p 151.

179. *Early Life*, p 156.

180. *Early Life*, p 173.

181. Thwaite, *Edmund Gosse: A Literary Landscape*, p 509.

182. Henry Nevinson, *Thomas Hardy* (P E N Books, London: 1941) p 12.

183. Edward Marsh, *A Number of People* (Heinemann, London: 1939).

184. *Early Life*, p 140.

185. Survey in *New Quarterly Magazine* (Oct 1879), in *Critical Heritage*, p 62.

186. Thomas Hardy, 'Why I Don't Write Plays', *Pall Mall Gazette* (31 Aug 1892), in *Public Voice*, pp 120–1.

187. *Early Life*, p 194.

188. *Early Life*, p 163.

189. *Early Life*, p 162.

190. *Early Life*, p 171.

191. *Early Life*, p 179.

192. *Early Life*, p 193.

193. Note transcribed by Florence Hardy, quoted in Millgate, *Thomas Hardy: A Biography Revisited*, p 211.

194. Richard L Purdy, *Thomas Hardy: A Bibliographical Study* (Clarendon Press, Oxford: 1954) p 44.

195. Thomas Hardy, *Two on a Tower*, ed Sally Shuttleworth (Penguin, London: 1999) p 57.

196. Havelock Ellis, 'Thomas Hardy's Novels', *Westminster Review* (Apr 1883), in *Critical Heritage*, p 132.

197. Ellis, 'Thomas Hardy's Novels', p 132.

198. Ellis, 'Thomas Hardy's Novels', pp 115, 125.

199. Ellis, 'Thomas Hardy's Novels', pp 116, 115, 120.

200. Thomas Hardy, 'General Preface to the Wessex Edition of 1912' in *Personal Writings*, p 46.

201. See Alun Howkins, *Reshaping Rural England, A Social History 1850–1925* (Harper Collins Academic, London: 1991), especially Chapter 1.

202. *Collected Letters*, vol 1, p 190.

203. T S Eliot, *On Poetry and Poets* (Faber & Faber, London: 1957) p 249. See also G M Young, *Portrait of an Age: Victorian England*, Second Edition (Oxford University Press, Oxford: 1953) p 146n.

204. Katharine Webb, letter to Sydney Cockerell (1920), quoted in Millgate, *Thomas Hardy: A Biography Revisited*, p 487.

205. Edmund Gosse, quoted in Millgate, *Thomas Hardy: A Biography Revisited*, p 222.

206. Noted in the diary of Edward Clodd, 1 October 1895; quoted in Millgate, *Thomas Hardy: A Biography Revisited*, p 326.

207. R R Bowker, *Harper's New Monthly Magazine* (Jun 1888), in Gibson (ed), *Interviews and Recollections*, p 13.

208. *Early Life*, p 231.

209. George Gissing, *London and the Life of Literature in Late Victorian England: The Diary of George Gissing, Novelist*, ed Pierre Coustillas (Brighton: Harvester Press, 1978) p 379.

210. *Early Life*, p 226.

211. John Newman and Nikolaus Pevsner, *The Buildings of England: Dorset* (Penguin, Harmondsworth: 1972) p 186.

212. Mabel Robinson, letter to I Cooper Willis, 17 Dec 1937 (Dorset County Museum); quoted in Millgate, *Thomas Hardy: A Biography Revisited*, p 276.

213. *Early Life*, p 210.

214. Quoted in Thwaite, *Edmund Gosse: A Literary Landscape*, p 333.

215. Mary Jeune, *Memories of Fifty Years* (Edward Arnold, London: 1909) p 210.

216. *Early Life*, p 179.

217. *Early Life*, p 220.

218. *Early Life*, p 225.

219. *Early Life*, p 241.

220. George Gissing, *The Collected Letters of George Gissing*, ed Paul Mattheisen *et al*, 8 vols (Ohio University Press, Athens, Ohio: 1990–6) vol 6, pp 27–8.

221. *Early Life*, p 191.

222. On the Home Rule crisis see *Early Life*, pp 232–4.

223. *Early Life*, p 268.

224. *Early Life*, p 268.

225. Edmund Gosse, 'The Influence of Democracy on Literature', *Contemporary Review* (Apr 1891) pp 523–36.

226. *Early Life*, p 309.

227. Thomas Hardy, 'The Dorsetshire Labourer', in *Public Voice*, p 50.

228. Hardy, 'The Dorsetshire Labourer', p 56.

229. Hardy, 'The Dorsetshire Labourer', p 56.

230. Hardy, 'The Dorsetshire Labourer', p 50.

231. *Tess of the D'Urbervilles*, p 238.

232. Thomas Hardy, *The Return of the Native*, ed Tony Slade (Penguin, London: 1999) p 12.

233. *Early Life*, p 157.

234. *Early Life*, p 230.

235. Irving Howe, *Thomas Hardy* (Weidenfeld and Nicolson, London: 1968) p 91.

236. Thomas Hardy, *The Mayor of Casterbridge*, ed Keith Wilson (Penguin, London: 1997) p 322.

237. *Early Life*, pp 197–8.

238. R H Hutton, *Spectator* (5 Jun 1886), in *Critical Heritage*, p 139.

239. *Early Life*, p 239.

240. Thomas Hardy, Tribute to William Dean Howells, *Harper's Weekly* (9 Mar 1912), in *Personal Writings*, p 246.

241. Thwaite, *Edmund Gosse: A Literary Landscape*, p 333.

242. *Early Life*, p 231.

243. R H Hutton, *Spectator* (5 Jun 1886), in *Critical Heritage*, p 139.

244. R H Hutton, *Spectator* (5 Jun 1886), in *Critical Heritage*, p 140.

245. *Early Life*, p 230.

246. R H Hutton, *Spectator* (5 Jun 1886), in *Critical Heritage*, p 142.

247. Thomas Hardy, *The Woodlanders*, ed Patricia Ingham (Penguin, London: 1998) p 278. Hereafter *The Woodlanders*.

248. *The Woodlanders*, p 8.

249. Edmund Gosse, 'Thomas Hardy', *The Speaker* (13 Sep 1890), in *Critical Heritage*, p 170.

250. Unsigned review of *Jude the Obscure*, *Athenaeum* (23 Nov 1895), *Critical Heritage*, p 251.

251. Unsigned review of *Desperate Remedies*, *Spectator* (22 Apr 1871), in *Critical Heritage*, p 4.

252. Unsigned review of *The Woodlanders* (Mar 1887), in *Critical Heritage*, p 141.

253. *Later Years*, p 16.

254. *Early Life*, p 199.

255. *The Woodlanders*, p 52.

256. *The Woodlanders,* pp 314, 331.

257. William Frederic Tillotson was proprietor of the *Bolton Weekly Journal*.

258. *Collected Letters*, vol 2, pp 216–17.

259. *Early Life*, p 239.

260. George Moore, *Literature at Nurse, or Circulating Morals* (Vizetelly, London: 1885).

261. Thomas Hardy, 'Candour in English Fiction', *New Review* (Jan 1890), in *Public Voice*, p 97.

262. *Collected Letters*, vol 1, p 196.

263. Richard L Purdy, *Thomas Hardy: A Bibliographical Study* (Clarendon Press, Oxford: 1954) p 72, hereafter Purdy, *Bibliographical Study*.

264. *Early Life*, p 291.

265. *Early Life*, p 230.

266. The novel's epigraph, 'Poor wounded name! My bosom as a bed / Shall lodge thee' is taken from Shakespeare's *Two Gentlemen of Verona* (I.ii.115–16).

267. Thomas Hardy, 'Heredity', in *Complete Poems*, p 434.

268. Thomas Hardy, *Tess of the D'Urbervilles*, ed Tim Dolin (Penguin, London: 1998) p 88.

269. Henry James, *Letters*, ed Leon Edel, 4 vols (The Belknap Press, Cambridge, Mass.: 1974) vol 1, p 194.

270. William Watson, *Academy* (6 Feb 1892), in *Critical Heritage*, p 197.

271. *Tess of the D'Urbervilles*, p 190.

272. *Collected Letters*, vol 1, p 254.

273. Mowbray Morris, *Quarterly Review* (Apr 1892) in *Critical Heritage*, pp 219, 221.

274. *Later Years*, p 7.

275. Margaret Higonnet, 'Introduction', *Tess of the D'Urbervilles*, ed Tim Dolin (Penguin, London: 1998), p xxii; *Collected Letters of Thomas Hardy*, vol 1, p 245.

276. *Later Years*, p 6.

277. *I, too, lost my heart to her as I went on with her history*: *Collected Letters*, vol 1, p 249.

278. *Early Life*, p 300.

279. Omitted by Florence Hardy from *Later Years*: see Thomas Hardy, *The Life and Work of Thomas Hardy*, ed Michael Millgate (Macmillan, London: 1984) p 258.

280. *Later Years*, p 18.

281. Thomas Hardy, 'A Broken Appointment' and 'At an Inn', in *Complete Poems*, pp 136, 68–9.

282. Thomas Hardy, 'Wessex Heights', in *Complete Poems*, pp 319–20.

283. Quoted in Millgate, *Thomas Hardy: A Biography Revisited*, p 286.

284. *Letters of Emma and Florence Hardy*, pp 7–8.

285. Purdy, *Bibliographical Study*, p 95.

286. *Early Life*, p 272.

287. Purdy, *Bibliographical Study*, p 89.

288. Thomas Hardy, *Jude the Obscure*, ed Dennis Taylor (Penguin, London: 1998) p 337, hereafter *Jude the Obscure*.

289. Thomas Hardy, 'Memoranda I', in *Personal Notebooks*, pp 6–7.

290. *Jude the Obscure*, p 23.

291. *Early Life*, p 285.

292. *Jude the Obscure*, p 244.

293. Penny Boumelha, *Thomas Hardy and Women: Sexual Ideology and Narrative Form* (Harvester Press, Brighton: 1982) p 138.

294. Holbrook Jackson, *The Eighteen Nineties*. The Life and Letters Series (1913; Jonathan Cape, London: 1931), p 72.

295. Jackson, *The Eighteen Nineties*, p 17.

296. *Jude the Obscure*, p 3.

297. *Collected Letters*, vol 2, p 206.

298. *Collected Letters*, vol 2, p 208.

299. *Later Years*, p 78.

300. Unsigned review of *Wessex Poems*, *Saturday Review* (7 Jan 1899), in *Critical Heritage*, p 319.

301. *Collected Letters*, vol 2, p 208.

302. *Later Years*, p 57.

303. Thomas Hardy, Preface to *Wessex Poems*, in *Complete Poems*, p 6.

304. *Later Years*, p 196.

305. Thomas Hardy, 'I Look into My Glass', *Complete Poems*, p 81.

306. Thomas Hardy, 'The Ivy-Wife', *Complete Poems*, p 57.

307. *Later Years*, p 178.

308. Thomas Hardy, 'In Time of "The Breaking of Nations"', in *Complete Poems*, p 543.

309. *Later Years*, p 178.
310. Hardy, *Collected Letters*, vol 2, p 233.
311. Hardy, *Collected Letters*, vol 2, p 233.
312. Thomas Hardy, 'At the War Office, London' and 'A Christmas Ghost-Story', in *Complete Poems*, pp 89–90, 90.
313. Hardy, *Collected Letters*, vol 2, p 280.
314. *Later Years*, p 97.
315. Thomas Hardy, 'The Darkling Thrush', in *Complete Poems*, p 150.
316. William Archer, *Real Conversations* (Heinemann, London: 1904) pp 46–7.
317. Thomas Hardy, 'In Tenebris, II', in *Complete Poems*, p 168.
318. Thomas Hardy, Preface to *Poems of the Past and Present*, in *Complete Poems*, p 84; Preface to *Jude the Obscure*, ed Dennis Taylor (Penguin, London: 1998) p 3.
319. *Early Life*, p 140.
320. John Wain, 'Introduction' to *The Dynasts* (Macmillan, London: 1965) p x.
321. *Later Years*, p 106.
322. Hardy, *Collected Letters*, vol 3, p 287.
323. Unsigned review of *Poems of the Past and Present, Saturday Review* (11 Jan 1902), in *Critical Heritage*, p 331.
324. Kenneth Rose, *King George V* (Weidenfeld and Nicolson, London: 1983) p 313.
325. Robert Graves, *Goodbye to All That*. 4th edition (1929. Penguin, Harmondsworth: 1960) p 251.
326. Thomas Hardy, 'The Going', in *Complete Poems*, p 338.
327. Thomas Hardy, 'The Going', in *Complete Poems*, p 339.
328. Benson diary, Magdalene College Library, Cambridge.
329. Hardy, *Collected Letters*, vol 5, p 232.
330. 'Only 5 (with varying dates 1871–98) give any evidence of earlier work': Purdy, *Bibliographical Study*, p 207. Purdy dates only 15 (of 159) from 1912–14.

331. Sydney Cockerell to Thomas Hardy, 7 Dec 1915 (Dorset County Museum).

332. *Letters of Emma and Florence Hardy*, p 114.

333. *Letters of Emma and Florence Hardy*, p 115.

334. *Letters of Emma and Florence Hardy*, p 113.

335. *Collected Letters of Thomas Hardy*, vol 5, p 214.

336. *Collected Letters*, vol 5, p 172.

337. Dorset County Museum.

338. See Thomas Hardy, *The Life and Work of Thomas Hardy*, ed Michael Millgate (Macmillan, London: 1984) p xiii.

339. George Moore, *Conversations in Ebury Street*. The Ebury Edition (1924; Heinemann, London: 1936), pp 76–85, p 84.

340. 'He Resolves to Say No More', in *Complete Poems*, pp 929–30.

341. 'Thomas Hardy's Wessex', *The Bookman* 1 (Oct 1891) p 26.

342. Martin J Wiener, *English Culture and the Decline of the Industrial Spirit* (Cambridge University Press, Cambridge: 1981) p 51.

343. Nicola J Watson, *The Literary Tourist: Readers and Places in Romantic and Victorian Britain* (Palgrave Macmillan, Basingstoke: 2006) p 192.

344. Peter Widdowson, *Hardy in History: A Study in Literary Sociology* (Routledge, London: 1989) p 61.

345. *Tess of the D'Urbervilles*, p 124.

346. Jonathan Crary, *Techniques of the Observer: On Vision and Modernity in the Nineteenth Century* (MIT Press, Cambridge, Mass.: 1990) p 10.

347. Thomas Hardy, 'The Dorsetshire Labourer', in *Public Voice*, p 50.

348. *Later Years*, p 9.

349. 'Afterwards', in *Complete Poems*, p 553.

| Year | Age | Life |
|------|-----|------|
| 1840 | | 2 June. Thomas Hardy born in Higher Bockhampton, Dorset, near Dorchester. |
| 1848–56 | 8–16 | Schooling in Stinsford (1848) and at Isaac Last's school in Dorchester. |
| 1856 | 16 | Witnesses hanging of Martha Brown.<br>Articled to Dorchester architect John Hicks (later assistant). |
| 1857 | 17 | Befriends Horace Moule, son of Henry Moule, vicar of Fordington, a major influence. |
| 1862 | 21 | Moves to London. Begins work for architect Arthur Blomfield in Adelphi Terrace. |
| 1865 | 25 | First publication, 'How I Built Myself a House', in *Chambers's Journal*. Begins *Studies, Specimens, &c.* notebook, and writing poetry. |
| 1867 | 27 | Returns to Dorset. Works on church restoration for Hicks. |
| 1868 | 28 | His first novel, *The Poor Man and the Lady*, rejected by Alexander Macmillan and his reader, John Morley, who are, however, both encouraging. |

| Year | History | Culture |
|------|---------|---------|
| *1840* | Marriage of Queen Victoria to Prince Albert. Ashes of Napoleon I returned to Paris. | Birth of Emile Zola. |
| *1848–56* | Revolutions of 1848 in Europe. Crimean War. | Foundation of Pre-Raphaelite Brotherhood. |
| *1856* | Outbreak of Anglo-Chinese War. | Flaubert, *Madame Bovary*. |
| *1857* | Indian Mutiny. Tsar Alexander II begins emancipation of Russian serfs. | George Eliot, *Scenes from Clerical Life*. Thomas Hughes, *Tom Brown's Schooldays*. |
| *1862* | American Civil War: Battles of 2nd Bull Run and Fredericksburg. Bismarck becomes Prussian prime minister. | Victor Hugo, *Les Misérables*. |
| *1865* | American Civil War ends. Death of Lord Palmerston. | Lewis Carroll, *Alice's Adventures in Wonderland*. |
| *1867* | Dominion of Canada established. | Anthony Trollope, *The Last Chronicle of Barset*. |
| *1868* | Abyssinian Expedition. Gladstone becomes Prime Minister. | Wilkie Collins, *The Moonstone*. Wagner, 'Die Meistersinger von Nürnberg'. |

| Year | Age | Life |
|------|-----|------|
| 1869 | 29 | Chapman and Hall accepts *The Poor Man and the Lady* but their reader, George Meredith, strongly advises Hardy against publishing, suggesting he try a story with 'more plot'. Smith, Elder and Co. also reject novel. Begins work for Weymouth architect Crickmay. |
| 1870 | 30 | Meets Emma Lavinia Gifford at rectory of St Juliot, north Cornwall, where he has been sent to assess restoration. |
| 1871 | 31 | Lays out £75 for *Desperate Remedies* to be published in three volumes by Tinsley Brothers. |
| 1872 | 32 | *Under the Greenwood Tree* (2 vols) published by Tinsley. Hardy moves from Weymouth to London for architectural work. |
| 1873 | 33 | *A Pair of Blue Eyes*, serialized in *Tinsley's Magazine*, published by Tinsley (3 vols). Horace Moule commits suicide. |
| 1874 | 34 | *Far from the Madding Crowd*, serialized in *Cornhill Magazine* (edited by Leslie Stephen), published by Smith, Elder (2 vols). Marries Emma Gifford; they live in Surbiton, London, and later move to Westbourne Grove, near Paddington. |
| 1875 | 35 | Move to Swanage, Dorset. |
| 1876 | 36 | *The Hand of Ethelberta*, serialized in *Cornhill Magazine*, published by Smith, Elder (2 vols). Hardys move to Yeovil in Somerset, then Sturminster Newton in Dorset. |

| Year | History | Culture |
|------|---------|---------|
| 1869 | Red River rebellion in Canada. Opening of the Suez Canal. Mohandas K Gandhi born. | R D Blackmore, *Lorna Doone*. Wagner, 'Rheingold'. |
| 1870 | Outbreak of Franco-Prussian War: Napoleon III defeated; Third Republic proclaimed in France. | Death of Charles Dickens. Delibes, 'Coppélia'. |
| 1871 | Proclamation of German Empire at Versailles. Paris Commune. | George Eliot, *Middlemarch*. Charles Darwin, *The Descent of Man*. |
| 1872 | Voting by secret ballot introduced in Britain. | Jules Verne, *Around the World in Eighty Days*. |
| 1873 | Death of Napoleon III in exile in England. | Walter Pater, *Studies in the History of the Renaissance*. |
| 1874 | Disraeli becomes Prime Minister. | Birth of G K Chesterton. Mussorgsky, 'Boris Godunov'. |
| 1875 | Britain buys shares in the Suez Canal. | Bizet, 'Carmen'. |
| 1876 | Alexander Graham bell invents the telephone. Ottoman sultan deposed. | Wagner, 'Siegfried'. |

| Year | Age | Life |
|------|-----|------|
| *1878* | 38 | *The Return of the Native*, serialized in *Belgravia Magazine*, published by Smith, Elder (3 vols). Moves to Tooting, London. *An Indiscretion in the Life of an Heiress* (adapted from part of *The Poor Man and the Lady*) serialized in *New Quarterly Magazine* and *Harper's Weekly*, New York. |
| *1880* | 40 | *The Trumpet-Major*, serialized in *Good Words* and *Demorest's Monthly Magazine*, published by Smith, Elder (3 vols). Seriously ill for much of year: dictates *A Laodicean* from sickbed. |
| *1881* | 41 | *A Laodicean*, serialized in *Harper's New Monthly Magazine*, published by Sampson Low (3 vols). Hardys leave London for Dorset |
| *1882* | 42 | *Two on a Tower*, serialized in *Atlantic Monthly*, published by Sampson Low (3 vols). Hardys at Wimborne. |
| *1883* | 43 | 'The Dorsetshire Labourer' published in *Longman's Magazine*. |
| *1885* | 45 | Hardys move from Shire-Hall Place Dorchester into Max Gate, the house designed by Hardy and built by Henry Hardy near Fordington Field just outside Dorchester. |
| *1886* | 46 | *The Mayor of Casterbridge*, serialized in the *Graphic*, published by Smith, Elder (2 vols). |
| *1887* | 47 | *The Woodlanders*, serialized in *Macmillan's Magazine*, published by Macmillan (3 vols). |
| *1888* | 48 | *Wessex Tales* published by Macmillan (2 vols). |

| Year | History | Culture |
|------|---------|---------|
| 1878 | End of Russo-Turkish War. Anti-Socialist law passed in Germany. | Algernon Charles Swinburne, *Poems and Ballads*. Ruskin-Whistler libel case. |
| 1880 | Gladstone succeeds Lord Beaconsfield (Disraeli) as Prime Minister. Electric lightbulb invented. | Death of George Eliot. Dostoevsy, *The Brothers Karamazov*. |
| 1881 | First Boer War. Flogging abolished in British armed forces. | Henry James, *Portrait of a Lady*. |
| 1882 | British occupy Cairo. Hiram Maxim patents his machine gun. | R L Stevenson, *Treasure Island*. Leslie Stephen, *Science of Ethics*. |
| 1883 | Bismarck introduces sickness insurance in Germany. Orient Express makes first run. | Death of Wagner. Nietzsche, *Thus Spake Zarathustra*. |
| 1885 | Death of General Gordon at Khartoum. First electric tram in England at Blackpool. | H Rider Haggard, *King Solomon's Mines*. Gilbert and Sullivan, 'The Mikado'. |
| 1886 | Gladstone introduces Irish Home Rule Bill | Henry James, *The Bostonians*. Rodin, 'The Kiss'. |
| 1887 | Queen Victoria's Golden Jubilee. | Arthur Conan Doyle, *A Study in Scarlet*. |
| 1888 | Kaiser Wilhelm II accedes to the throne. 'Jack the Ripper' murders in London. | Rudyard Kipling, *Plain Tales from the Hills*. Oscar Wilde, *The Happy Prince, and Other Tales*. |

| Year | Age | Life |
|------|-----|------|
| *1890* | 50 | 'Candour in English Fiction' published in *New Review*. |
| *1891* | 51 | *A Group of Noble Dames* (story collection) published by Osgood, McIlvaine (1 vol). *Tess of the d'Urbervilles*, serialized in expurgated form in the *Graphic*, published by Osgood, McIlvaine (3 vols). |
| *1892* | 52 | Hardy's father dies. *The Pursuit of the Well-Beloved* serialized in the *Illustrated London News*. *Our Exploits at West Poley*, a boys' story, begins serialization in Boston in the *Household*. |
| *1893* | 53 | Meets and falls in love with Florence Henniker. |
| *1894* | 54 | *Life's Little Ironies* (story collection) published by Osgood, McIlvaine (1 vol). 'The Spectre of the Real', written in collaboration with Florence Henniker, published. |
| *1895* | 55 | *Jude the Obscure*, serialized in *Harper's New Monthly Magazine*, published by Osgood, McIlvaine (1 vol). 'The Wessex Novels', the first uniform collected edition of Hardy's fiction, begin publication by Osgood, McIlvaine |
| *1897* | 57 | *The Pursuit of the Well-Beloved* extensively revised as *The Well-Beloved* and published by Osgood, McIlvaine (1 vol). |
| *1898* | 58 | Hardy's first collection of poetry, *Wessex Poems and Other Verses*, published by Harper and Brothers. Includes illustrations by Hardy. |

| Year | History | Culture |
|------|---------|---------|
| 1890 | Bismarck dismissed by Wilhelm II. | Oscar Wilde, *The Picture of Dorian Gray*. |
| 1891 | Kaiser Wilhelm II visits London.<br>Tranby-Croft baccarat scandal. | Rudyard Kipling, *The Light that Failed*. |
| 1892 | Gladstone returns as Prime Minister. | Oscar Wilde, *Lady Windermere's Fan*.<br>Tchaikovsky, 'The Nutcracker'. |
| 1893 | Independent Labour Party formed.<br>Franco-Russian alliance signed. | Oscar Wilde, *A Woman of No Importance*. |
| 1894 | Sino-Japanese War.<br>Death duties (inheritance tax) introduced in Britain. | G and W Grossmith, *Diary of a Nobody*.<br>Anthony Hope, *The Prisoner of Zenda*. |
| 1895 | Trail and imprisonment of Oscar Wilde.<br>Chinese defeated by Japanese. | H G Wells, *The Time Machine*.<br>W B Yeats, *Poems*. |
| 1897 | Graeco-Turkish War.<br>Russia occupies Port Arthur.<br>Queen Victoria's Diamond Jubilee. | Joseph Conrad, *The Nigger of the Narcissus*.<br>Havelock Ellis, *Studies in the Psychology of Sex*. |
| 1898 | British reconquer the Sudan, avenging General Gordon.<br>Spanish-American War. | H G Wells, *The War of the Worlds*.<br>Oscar Wilde, *The Ballad of Reading Gaol*. |

| Year | Age | Life |
|------|-----|------|
| *1899* | 59 | Begins as a 'public poet', publishing poems in newspapers in response to the outbreak of the Boer War. |
| *1901* | 61 | *Poems of the Past and the Present* published by Harper and Brothers. |
| *1904* | 64 | Jemima Hardy dies. Part I of *The Dynasts*, Hardy's 'Iliad' of the Napoleonic Wars, published by his new publisher, Macmillan. |
| *1905* | 65 | Meets Florence Emily Dugdale, who becomes his secretary, and will become his second wife. |
| *1906* | 66 | *The Dynasts*, Part II. |
| *1908* | 68 | *The Dynasts*, Part III. |
| *1909* | 69 | *Time's Laughingstocks, and Other Verses* |
| *1910* | 70 | Awarded the Order of Merit. Receives the Freedom of the Borough of Dorchester |

| Year | History | Culture |
| --- | --- | --- |
| 1899 | Outbreak of Second Boer War: British defeats at Stormberg, Magersfontein and Colenso. First Peace Conference at The Hague. | Rudyard Kipling, *Stalky and Co.* Elgar, 'Enigma Variations'. |
| 1901 | Death of Queen Victoria Second Boer War: Boers begin guerilla warfare. | Thomas Mann, *Buddenbrooks.* |
| 1904 | Outbreak of Russo-Japanese War. | Death of Leslie Stephen. G K Chesterton, *The Napoleon of Notting Hill.* |
| 1905 | Russo-Japanese War: Japanese take Port Arthur and destroy Russian fleet at Tsushima. Tangier Crisis. | E M Forster, *Where Angels Fear to Tread.* Baroness Orczy, *The Scarlet Pimpernel.* |
| 1906 | Algeciras Conference. | John Galsworthy, *The Silver Box.* |
| 1908 | Asquith becomes Prime Minister, with Lloyd George as Chancellor. 'Young Turk' revolt. | Kenneth Grahame, *The Wind in the Willows.* |
| 1909 | State visits by Edward VII to Berlin and Rome. First cross-Channel flight by Blériot. | Matisse, 'The Dance'. |
| 1910 | George V succeeds Edward VII. Dr Crippen executed for murder of his wife. | E M Forster, *Howard's End.* Stravinsky, 'The Firebird'. |

| Year | Age | Life |
|------|-----|------|
| *1912* | 72 | Emma Hardy dies unexpectedly. Hardy, grief-stricken and remorseful, writes a series of love lyrics that will become the elegy, 'Poems of 1912–13'. |
| *1913* | 73 | *A Changed Man and Other Tales.* |
| *1914* | 74 | Marries Florence Dugdale. *Satires of Circumstance, Lyrics, and Reveries. The Dynasts: Prologue and Epilogue* privately printed. |
| *1915* | 75 | Hardy's beloved sister Mary dies; and his cousin Frank George, a possible heir, is killed at Gallipoli. |
| *1916* | 76 | *Selected Poems.* |
| *1917* | 77 | *Moments of Vision and Miscellaneous Verses.* Hardy and Florence begin sorting papers and making notes for the posthumously published biography, mostly authored by Hardy himself. |
| *1919* | 79 | The deluxe Macmillan 'Mellstock Edition' of Hardy's work begins. |
| *1922* | 82 | *Late Lyrics and Earlier with Many Other Verses.* |
| *1923* | 83 | *The Famous Tragedy of the Queen of Cornwall* (drama). |
| *1925* | 85 | *Human Shows, Far Phantasies, Songs and Trifles.* |

| Year | History | Culture |
|------|---------|---------|
| 1912 | War breaks out in the Balkans. Amundsen beats Captain Scott to the South Pole. | J M Synge, *The Playboy of the Western World*. |
| 1913 | End of Balkan War. Suffragette demonstrations in Britain. | D H Lawrence, *Sons and Lovers*. |
| 1914 | Outbreak of the First World War: Battle of Mons, Battle of the Marne, First Battle of Ypres. | James Joyce, *Dubliners*. Edgar Rice Burroughs, *Tarzan of the Apes*. |
| 1915 | First World War: Gallipoli campaign; battles of Neuve Chapelle and Loos. | John Buchan, *The Thirty-Nine Steps*. W Somerset Maugham, *Of Human Bondage*. |
| 1916 | First World War: Battles of Verdun and the Somme. Battle of Jutland. | George Moore, *The Brook Kerith*. Film: *Intolerance*. |
| 1917 | First World War: Battle of Passchendaele. October Revolution in Russia. | T S Eliot, *Prufrock and Other Observations*. Alec Waugh, *The Loom of Youth*. |
| 1919 | Versailles Peace Conference. | First of Hugh Lofting's 'Dr Doolittle' stories. |
| 1922 | Mussolini's march on Rome: forms fascist government. | T S Eliot, *The Waste Land*. Film: *Nosferatu*. |
| 1923 | Failed coup in Munich by Adolf Hitler's Nazis. | P G Wodehouse, *The Inimitable Jeeves*. |
| 1925 | Hitler reorganizes Nazi Party and publishes *Mein Kampf*. | Noel Coward, *Hay Fever*. F Scott Fitzgerald, *The Great Gatsby*. |

| Year | Age | Life |
|------|-----|------|
| *1928* | 87 | 11 January: Thomas Hardy dies. His heart is buried in the grave he intended to share with Emma Hardy at Stinsford. His ashes are buried in Poet's Corner, Westminster Abbey. *Winter Words in Various Moods and Metres* published posthumously. |

| Year | History | Culture |
|------|---------|---------|
| *1928* | Kellogg-Briand Pact. Discovery of penicillin. | Evelyn Waugh, *Decline and Fall*. Virginia Woolf, *Orlando*. |

# Further Reading

**Works by Thomas Hardy**

The most reliable paperback editions of Hardy's novels are those published by Penguin Classics (general editor Patricia Ingham), which mostly use the first volume editions of the novels as copytexts, and the Oxford World's Classics series (general editor Simon Gatrell).

The poems are widely available. The two standard editions are *The Complete Poems*, ed James Gibson (Macmillan, London: 1976), and the five-volume *The Complete Poetical Works of Thomas Hardy*, ed Samuel Hynes (Clarendon Press, Oxford: 1982–95). The latter contains *The Dynasts*. The best paperback selections are *Thomas Hardy: Selected Poems*, Longman Annotated Texts, ed Tim Armstrong (Longman, London: 1993) and *Thomas Hardy: Selected Poetry and Non-Fictional Prose*, ed Peter Widdowson (Macmillan, Basingstoke: 1997).

**Hardy's Letters, Notebooks, and Personal and Public Writings**

Hardy was not a great letter-writer; nevertheless *The Collected Letters of Thomas Hardy*, ed Richard L Purdy and Michael Millgate, 7 vols (Clarendon Press, Oxford: 1978–88) make fascinating reading. Beautifully edited, with a very useful index. Millgate has also edited *Letters of Emma and Florence Hardy* (Clarendon Press, Oxford: 1996).

Millgate's scrupulous edition of *Thomas Hardy's Public Voice: The Essays, Speeches, and Miscellaneous Prose* (Clarendon Press, Oxford: 2001) collects Hardy's essays (including 'The Dorsetshire Labourer' and 'Candour in English Fiction') along with speeches, newspapers items and other public utterances. Many of these items were also included in Harold Orel's collection, *Thomas Hardy's Personal Writings* (Macmillan, London: 1996), which usefully gathers together the prefaces Hardy wrote for his novels and poems.

*The Early Life of Thomas Hardy, 1840–1891* (Macmillan, London: 1928) and *The Later Years of Thomas Hardy, 1892–1928* (Macmillan, London: 1930) were published under Florence Hardy's name but were substantially written by Hardy himself. They were amalgamated into a single volume, *The Life of Thomas Hardy* (Macmillan, London: 1962). Confusingly, the two-volume first edition was reprinted from the original plates and also published in a single volume as *The Life of Thomas Hardy* by Studio Editions, London in 1994. Michael Millgate returned to the typescripts to produce a Hardy-only edition (i.e. without Florence Hardy's additions and deletions), *The Life and Work of Thomas Hardy* (Macmillan, Basingstoke: 1984).

Hardy burned many of his notebooks as he was writing the *Early Life* and *Later Years* after 1917. Others were destroyed at his request after his death. A number survived, however, including the absorbing *Literary Notebooks of Thomas Hardy*, ed Lennart Bjork, 2 vols (Macmillan, London: 1985), containing annotated transcribed excerpts from articles in magazines and books: a detailed picture of Hardy's reading and thinking over a long period. *The Personal Notebooks of Thomas Hardy*, ed Richard H Taylor (Macmillan, London: 1979) collects a number of miscellaneous shorter notebooks, including the crucial early 'Memoranda', and the 'Schools of Painting Notebook' from the London years. Most intriguing of all is *Thomas Hardy's Studies, Specimens &c. Notebook*, ed Pamela Dalziel and Michael Millgate (Clarendon Press, Oxford:

1994), where Hardy experimented with poetic form in the 1860s. *Thomas Hardy's 'Facts' Notebook: A Critical Edition*, ed William Greenslade (Ashgate, Aldershot: 2004) reproduces the notebook he used to record facts from old copies of the *Dorset County Chronicle* in Dorchester in the mid-1880s.

Readers interested in exploring the rich manuscript holdings of Hardyana at the Dorset County Museum can do so through the 18-reel microfilm edition of *The Original Manuscripts and Papers of Thomas Hardy* (EP Microform, East Ardsley, Yorkshire: 1975), widely available in libraries.

## Bibliographies

The standard bibliography remains Richard L Purdy's *Thomas Hardy: A Bibliographical Study* (Clarendon Press, Oxford: 1954). A useful (though incomplete) bibliographical guide to manuscript sources is the *Index of English Literary Manuscripts 1800–1900 Part 2: Hardy-Lamb*, ed Barbara Rosenbaum (Mansell, New York: 1990). See also Millgate's *Thomas Hardy's Library at Max Gate: Catalogue of an Attempted Reconstruction* at http://www.library. utoronto.ca/fisher/hardy/.

For bibliographies of works about Hardy, see Helmut E Gerber and W Eugene Davis's thorough 2-volume *Thomas Hardy: An Annotated Bibliography of Writings About Him* (Northern Illinois University Press, De Kalb: 1973, 1983). The online Thomas Hardy Association keeps a regularly updated 'checklist' of current works (since 2000). Visit http://www.yale.edu/hardysoc/Welcome/ welcomet.htm.

## Biographies and memoirs

The standard scholarly biography is Michael Millgate's indispensable *Thomas Hardy: A Biography Revisited* (Oxford University Press, Oxford: 2004), revised from his 1982 *Thomas Hardy: A Biography*. Claire Tomalin's *Thomas Hardy: The Time-Torn Man*

(Viking, London: 2006), while it adds nothing much in the way of new knowledge, sensitively captures its elusive subject. Martin Seymour-Smith's much maligned *Hardy* (Bloomsbury, London: 1994) takes a rather barmy set against rival Hardy authorities (especially Millgate) and its over-familiarity with the diffident 'Tom' is irksome, but it contains some fine insights and analysis of the works. Robert Gittings's *Young Thomas Hardy* and *Thomas Hardy's Later Years* (Heinemann, London: 1975, 1978) are still well worth reading, even if they are intent on taking Hardy down a peg or two.

For memoirs of Hardy, consult Emma Hardy's *Some Recollections* (Oxford University Press, Oxford: 1979), *Thomas Hardy: Interviews and Recollections*, ed James Gibson (Macmillan, Basingstoke: 1999), and *Thomas Hardy Remembered*, ed Martin Ray (Ashgate, Aldershot: 2007).

## Wessex

Hardy's creation of Wessex is traced in Simon Gatrell's *Thomas Hardy's Vision of Wessex* (Macmillan, Basingstoke: 2003). On Wessex geography see H C Darby, 'The Regional Geography of Hardy's Wessex', *Geographical Review*, 38 (1948) pp 426–43 and John Barrell, 'Geographies of Hardy's Wessex', *Journal of Historical Geography*, 8 (1982) pp 347–61. Denys Kay-Robinson's *Hardy's Wessex Reappraised* (David and Charles, Newton Abbot: 1972) was the first reassessment of Hermann Lea's incomplete and sometimes erroneous survey of Hardy's topographical sources in *Thomas Hardy's Wessex* (1913; Macmillan, London: 1977). The afterlife of Hardy's Wessex as a tourist destination has not yet been fully surveyed, although brief accounts, like that in Nicola J Watson's *The Literary Tourist: Readers and Places in Romantic and Victorian Britain* (Palgrave Macmillan, Basingstoke: 2006) have made a start.

## Critical Studies

Hardy criticism begins with the first reviews and essays, collected in *Thomas Hardy: The Critical Heritage*, ed R G Cox (Routledge & Kegan Paul, London: 1970). The recommended companions and reference guides are: Dale Kramer (ed), *The Cambridge Companion to Thomas Hardy* (Cambridge University Press, Cambridge: 1999), a collection of essays covering Hardy's life and work; Norman Page's *Oxford Reader's Companion to Hardy* (Oxford University Press, Oxford: 2000), a very handy reference book with contributions by the leading authorities; and Ruth A Firor's still fascinating *Folkways in Thomas Hardy* (University of Pennsylvania Press, Philadelphia: 1931), a detailed descriptive account of superstition and lore in Hardy. The analysis of Hardy's texts and their publishing history has provoked some valuable work, too: see Simon Gatrell, *Hardy, the Creator: A Textual Biography* (Clarendon Press, Oxford: 1988), Patricia Ingham, 'The Evolution of *Jude the Obscure*', *Review of English Studies*, 27 (1976), and J T Laird, *The Shaping of 'Tess of the d'Urbervilles'* (Clarendon Press, Oxford: 1975).

Hardy studies flourished in the late 1960s and early 1970s with the publication of Irving Howe's *Thomas Hardy* (Weidenfeld and Nicolson, London: 1968), J Hillis Miller's *Thomas Hardy: Distance and Desire* (The Belknap Press of Harvard University Press, Cambridge, Mass: 1970), Jean R Brooks's *Thomas Hardy: The Poetic Structure* (Elek Books, London: 1971), Michael Millgate's *Thomas Hardy: His Career as a Novelist* (The Bodley Head, London: 1971) and Ian Gregor's *The Great Web: the Form of Hardy's Major Fiction* (Faber, London: 1974).

The complexity of Hardy's class position and its significance to his work inform a number of very important books, including: Raymond Williams, *The Country and the City* (Chatto and Windus, London: 1973); Terry Eagleton, *Criticism and Ideology: A Study in Marxist Literary Theory* (Verso, London: 1978); John Goode, *Thomas Hardy: The Offensive Truth* (Blackwell, Oxford: 1988);

Peter Widdowson, *Hardy in History: A Study in Literary Sociology* (Routledge, London: 1989); Roger Ebbatson, *Hardy: The Margin of the Unexpressed* (Sheffield Academic Press, Sheffield: 1993); and Joe Fisher, *The Hidden Hardy* (Macmillan, London: 1992).

The centrality of women in Hardy's work has attracted some very fine feminist studies. The best are Penny Boumelha, *Thomas Hardy and Women: Sexual Ideology and Narrative Form* (Harvester Press, Brighton: 1982), Patricia Ingham, *Thomas Hardy. Feminist Readings* (Harvester Wheatsheaf, London: 1989), and the essays collected in Margaret R Higonnet (ed), *The Sense of Sex: Feminist Perspectives on Hardy* (University of Illinois Press, Urbana: 1993).

Hardy's poetry has been the subject of numerous books, chapters and articles, of which the following are some of the best: Donald Davie's *Thomas Hardy and British Poetry* (Routledge & Kegan Paul, London: 1973); Tom Paulin's *Thomas Hardy: The Poetry of Perception* (Macmillan, London: 1975); and Dennis Taylor's *Hardy's Poetry, 1860–1928* (Macmillan, London: 1981).

# Picture Sources

The author and publishers wish to express their thanks to the following sources of illustrative material and/or permission to reproduce it. They will make proper acknowledgements in future editions in the event that any omissions have occurred.

# Index

NB All family relationships
are to Thomas Hardy, unless
otherwise stated.
For Hardy's works, see under
'Hardy, Thomas'.

## A
Abercorn, Duchess of 85
Alma-Tadema, Lawrence 73, 85
Arnold, Matthew 41, 65, 73, 85,
    101

## B
Barnes, Revd William 26
Bastow, Henry Robert 24, 26
Beardsley, Aubrey 101
Bernhardt, Sarah 106
Besant, Walter 72, 92, 99
Birkerts, Sven 2
Blackmore, R D 64
Blomfield, Arthur 31
Blomfield, Charles James 31
Blunden, Edmund 130
Braddon, Mary Elizabeth 43, 70
Broderick, Lady Hilda 85
Brooke, Rupert 7
Browne, Martha 16

Browning, Robert 72

## C
Caine, Hall 92
Campbell, Mrs Patrick 106
Carr, J Comyns 76
Carnarvon, Countess of 85
Chesterton, G K 7, 137
Clodd, Edward 126, 135
Cockerell, Sydney 134, 138
Collins, Wilkie 43
Corelli, Marie 92
Crickmay, G R 46, 48

## D
Darwin, Charles 6, 39
De La Mare, Walter 130
Dickens, Charles 29–30, 43
Douglas, Sir George 110
Downton, Lizzie 10
Dugdale, Eva (2nd wife's sister)
    137
Dugdale, Florence Emily *see*
    Florence Emily Hardy

## E
Edward, Prince of Wales 128–9